things to make with paper

things to make with paper

187 FUN PROJECTS

DON MUNSON and ALLIANORA ROSSE

GALAHAD BOOKS · NEW YORK

Published by arrangement with
Charles Scribner's Sons. Formerly published
under the title *The Paper Book*.
Copyright © 1970 Allianora Rosse and Don Munson

Printed in the United States of America
Library of Congress Catalog Card Number: 73-89244
ISBN: 0-88365-107-6

CONTENTS

FOREWORD

A whole new world is waiting for those with the imagination to create it. Here are the signs and portents, hints, clues, and the directions in some cases, for the creation of paper-art. This art, and craft, ranges all the way from innocence to sophistication, all the way from the Pentagon to kindergarten and back. This is the paper world.

Paper is one of our most readily available materials, and we can make of it what we will. We can make airplanes, art objects such as mobiles and origami; silhouettes, collages; doll houses, playhouses; and useful things, such as aprons, place mats, meat ruffs and *cachepots*.

PREFACE

Whenever the authors speak of making something out of paper, and snip away to demonstrate, the reaction is the same—silence. Everybody has gone looking for scissors. If someone has even a smidgeon of the creative urge, paper-art will bring it out. A fascination asserts itself in the transforming of such simple materials (paper, cardboard and things that clutter most people's houses) into something beautiful, or even useful.

On its higher levels paper-art is for adults, though children enjoy it and learn from it in their early years. Kindergarten children and distinguished architects build their dream cities of paper, and so do the men who build our rockets to the moon.

None of the visitors to the Pentagon is surprised when, climbing the tower-like staircase, he is assailed by a tiny paper plane, a plane scissored and stuck together reasonably close to the principles of advanced aerodynamics.

Aesthetics and psychology frequently cross paths in the area of paper-art. Such noted artists as Alexander Calder find it useful in developing a concept. Psychologists value it because it calls for complete concentration, and perhaps equally because pride in accomplishment is healing to the damaged ego.

On the social level, paper-art is rapidly becoming the In Thing. As charades were once big in social life because they dignified simple play with an intellectual aura, this burgeoning new art dignifies simple play with an intellectual and an aesthetic aura.

Two well-known aeronautical scientists are known for never going to a party without paper, scissors, and sticky tape; for making a point of going to the same parties; and for starting competitions to see whose model will fly the better. One of their competitors has said that new concepts have come out of such cocktail-party rivalry.

At many such a party there are people who know nothing about Newton except that he showed unusual interest in apples, little about Rembrandt except chiaroscuro, and about Socrates only that he met such a sad and untimely death; yet these people are right in the thick of things when the scissors and paper appear.

Educators, psychologists, and sociologists have long urged toys, games, and crafts that call for participation on the part of the child. Children are not so inert as toy-manufacturers believe because after a brief period of fascination with their manufactured toys, they may tear them to pieces. Whether they do this for fun or in anger, nobody is quite sure. But perceptive parents are learning to work with their children in creating their own toys. Something that has come out of your own mind and feeling, and which you have worked on devotedly, you do not destroy.

Between the extremes of paper-art—the scientists who, dealing in scientific abstractions, fly their planes in the Pentagon, and the children who develop their creativity—lies an equally important group, the people who insist upon making their lives and their homes individual, instead of buying the mass-produced home furnishings. Such individualists will always want to do it their own way, and are always interested in such guidelines as we find here with respect to furnishing the house, decorating its exterior, and making the entertainment more interesting. These individualists may well find interest in the Table of Contents where the listings point the way to individual ways of doing things, and open up a grand prospect for exploration.

Of course you can buy all these things: lanterns, lamp shades, window pictures, dresses, costumes, masks, baskets, boxes, flowers, trees, plants, and a hundred others, but if we bought them we would all have the same things as the people in the houses on either side of us, and the people across the street.

Do we not marry because we think we are uniquely designed for each other, and do we not wish to live together in a house that is unique? We do. Let us then design our houses to reflect our own tastes and personalities.

There is a listing of the supplies and tools that may be used. While most of the creations call for only paper and glue and colors such as we usually have around the house, none calls for more exotic materials than are available at drug stores, stationery stores, and art supply shops.

As in an art class with twenty students looking at the same still life or model, and each producing a different result, so it is with scissors and paper. The work of each paper artist will reflect his personality. Whether a success or a failure, it will be his own creation.

How to describe the adventure? Perhaps as that of semi-skilled fliers who are given instruction and compass directions and sent off into the sky. Each will, perhaps, reach a different destination, and some will make very happy landings.

ILLUSTRATOR'S FOREWORD

It is my intention to make paper art seem easy. All of the items are rather basic and certainly nothing in the book is too difficult for anyone to make. Then, too, you can invent new objects that express your own individuality. Similar objects can be made to look entirely different by using different types of paper, different colors and prints on the papers, etcetera.

I have refrained from using measurements as much as possible in order to give the reader liberty to vary the design; also to eliminate much calculating and measuring. Where measurements are important I have so indicated; otherwise I have just given a suggestion of about how much paper to use or how much board to cut. Most of the measurements given are indicated in the illustrations.

I have tried to illustrate each step in the making of each object. But don't be discouraged if things don't go right at first. If a certain paper does not fit your requirements, try another one. Usually not much time will be lost, and you will be more satisfied with the results. If you are planning to use an extravagant paper or one of exquisite beauty, be sure you know what you are going to do before you cut or glue. It is sometimes worthwhile to follow instructions with a piece of paper of little value, such as brown paper, newsprint or typewriter paper, just to get the feel of what you will be doing.

One thing that should be kept in mind at all times is neatness. Lines should be straight when called for, squares should be really square, and circles should be real circles. Also, use of proper tools is important—sharp cutting knives and good paper shears. It is possible to make paper objects with dull tools, but it does not result in neat work and the end products are not as attractive.

Use good glue and never too much. Always be prepared to wipe up excess glue. Always have a saucer with a damp sponge on hand and a roll of paper towels for spillage and also to keep your fingers free of glue. Another hint for gluing: If you think printed papers will be easily damaged by the dampness of the glue, then only put the glue on the opposite surface to be glued.

There are all kinds of paper available. And most come in brilliant colors, which can be combined in so many ways that decorations are almost unnecessary. And then there are the incredibly varied printed papers. Most of these are of a quality and thickness that make them suitable for many uses.

Following is a list of papers, tools, and other materials that I believe are the most suitable for making any of the objects in this book.

PAPERS (thin)
Tissue paper
Crepe paper
Rice paper
Coated paper
Cellophane
Bond paper
Vellum tracing paper
Wrapping and gift-wrap paper (printed and plain)

PAPERS (heavy)
Drawing paper
Thinnest bristol board
Velour paper
Metallic paper (heavy not so much in terms of weight as in nature of handling)
Construction paper
Blotter paper
Kraft paper (bags, etc.)
Paper cloth

BOARDS (thin)
Lightweight cardboard
Bristol board
Poster board
Light-weight illustration board

BOARDS (heavy)
Double and triple weight cardboard
Single- and double-sided corrugated board and cartons
Heavy-weight corrugated cardboard (hard)
Chipboard

TOOLS (Cutlery)
Long paper shears for straight cutting
Paper shears for heavy cutting
Small scissors for fine cutting (such as nail and cuticle scissors)
Very sharp cutting knife (frisket, whittling, or razor blade)
Dull knife for scoring (a letter opener will serve)
Hole puncher
Awl

MEASURING EQUIPMENT
Squares and rulers
Tape measure
Metal yard stick (very useful to guide a blade in cutting)
Compass

GLUES
Library glue
Rubber cement (not suitable for long-lasting hold)
UHU (a strong-holding rubber cement)
Duco (has the advantage of being transparent)
Elmer's and other white glues (the best for most paper work)

TAPES
Sticky tapes of the transparent and near-transparent types
Double-faced transparent tape (useful for covering boxes)

Passe partout (an opaque colored paper tape)
Mystik tape or other cloth tape
Gummed paper tape
Reinforced packing tape

MISCELLANEOUS
Erasers

MISCELLANEOUS (CONT.)

Needles
Paper clips, pins, and clothespins
Thread and string
Elastics
Paints and felt-tip marking pens

Most of the papers are readily available at art supply stores, others at paper supply houses (see the Yellow Pages), stationery stores, gift shops, drug stores, department stores, and greeting card stores. Grocery stores and liquor stores are usually generous with cartons. Large pieces of corrugated board can be found in well-supplied art stores, and other special materials can be found in lumber yards.

TECHNIQUES

Curling: To curl use fairly thin paper, bending a strip of it over the edge of a dull knife or the back of a knife and pull it over the edge with one hand while the thumb of the other hand is maintaining tension.

Curving: Heavier papers can be curved by holding both ends of the paper and running the paper over the edge of a board or table edge firmly and evenly.

Cutting and multiple cutting: This can be done best with sharp equipment (be it knife or scissors) to get best results. Multiple cutting is cutting the same design or outline through several layers of paper. Fold paper accordion fashion into layers, as many as you wish. Draw or otherwise indicate the design on the top layer, and cut out.

Scoring and folding: Score by pressing down on lines to be bent or folded with a dull knife. This pressure will break the surface tension of the paper, making it easy to bend or fold along the desired lines. The scoring may follow any course, straight or curved.

To make cones: Make a circle, and cut one radius (anywhere), bring one end over the other for about one-eighth inch and fasten with staple or glue. (A) is the widest cone. By taking smaller sections of the circle, one is able to make smaller cones: one-half (B), one-third (C) and one-fourth (D).

things to make with paper

CHAPTER 1

PAPER PLANES, KITES AND BOATS

If the designing of paper airplanes sounds like children's work, this impression must be corrected at once. Many concepts of aeronautics derive from the study of paper planes. These tiny craft, products of play and of dreams, are forerunners of achievements with respect to airplanes and also rockets to the moon.

My own acquaintance with paper airplanes started when I met Joe Maynard, who was helping the U. S. Army fight its way up through Italy. He then was transferred to radio-telegraph duty atop a lighthouse in the Tyrrhenian Sea south of Genoa. Since the usual masculine recreations were restricted in this all-male environment, Joe and his buddies, after agonized reappraisals, realized that they had an unparalleled opportunity to study aeronautics. Genoa was a mile away; what if on a clear day with the wind right you could land a paper plane on the Genoa beach? Who thought he could do it, and who would like to bet on it?

Never were so many planes launched with so few reaching their destination. But what a moment of triumph when one landed on the sand.

Not nearly so colorful was the time on Newbury Street in Boston, where Joe Maynard and I toiled at an advertising agency. The locale was ideally suited to challenge designers of paper planes. Our windows were on the third floor, and the buildings across the street were six stories high. What a *scientific* triumph it would be to design a plane, launch it, and see it rise across the narrow street and scale the opposite buildings.

Maynard and I competed relentlessly between ugly intrusions by people interested in advertising, and there were occasional triumphs, thanks partly to our talent, and perhaps more thanks on the hotter days to magnificent thermals rising from the pavement of Newbury Street. Whichever it was, we saw a few of our planes reconnoiter near the ominous buildings opposite, scale the ramparts, and fly off to Copley Square and glory.

Staunch men and true build and fly paper airplanes. Let anyone who looks down on the art, design and fly three models. If just one of them is air-worthy, you have a convert. Special interest is shown by airplane designers or manu-

1

facturers, and increasingly by people who seek new outlets for their talents and a chance for the kind of complete concentration that takes them far away from their worries.

If a professional designer's real model crashes, he goes back to the drawing board with incalculable losses in money and blood. The paper-flyer goes back to his scissors and paper with only a little damage to his pride, and a compensating boost to his determination. He studies the spread of the wings, the straightness of the spine, the camber, which involves bending the leading edges of wings down and trailing edges up, the weight-spread, and wonders how he failed. Perhaps the wings were so wide as to lose proper rigidity; perhaps the wing assembly was so far from the tail as to lose balance; perhaps there was too much weight on the nose or the tail. You trim a little here and bend a little there, and try again. What an excitement when your paper model flies off like a million-dollar plane! It is no copy of anyone else's paper plane. It is *your plane*.

Novices in the art of paper airplaning should come to understand that they are not beginning an endeavor for which they will find exact instruction and produce exact results. Their acceptance to the brotherhood is tentative. In the view of this brotherhood, once you have a few clues, it remains for you to demonstrate that you are worthy of membership. Exact measurements as to length of fusilage, wing-spread—and that kind of thing—have more to do with manufacture than experimenting, and paper-flying is wholly experimental.

Only those who have actually experienced the magic of the first lift-off—whether of a paper plane or any other kind—will ever be able to understand flying. Though paper engineers concern themselves with wing and tail relationships, rigidity, thermals, and all the rest, they like all aeronautical engineers know that full knowledge waits upon the take-off—and the landing.

One of the greatest paper airplanes ever built (besides those Maynard and I launched over Newbury Street) was designed by Navy Captain R. S. Barnaby of Philadelphia. At the 1966-67 First International Airplane Convention Capt. Barnaby's little craft flew better than 12,000 other entries. How a plane flies is the ultimate test. It may be brilliantly designed and beautiful, but the final test is performance.

MAKING PLANES THAT FLY

The first step in making a plane is to fold a sheet of paper (8½ x 11 bond perhaps, or something with a little starch in it) in half vertically (a). Trying different paper is part of the adventure, but it must be stiff enough so that the wings do not droop.

To make Maynard's plane, which is perhaps the simplest and in some ways

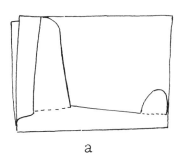

a

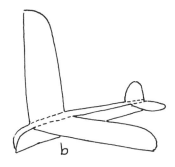

b

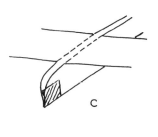

c

the best, involves cutting a half-inch nose parallel to the fold, and then curving away with the scissors to shape the wings, then curving back to the spine to within half an inch, before turning toward the tail (b). The tail assembly should be about an eighth of the wing assembly.

Next, fold the wings and tail fins back to the fusilage (c) and then bring them up until they're at right angles to it, pinning them at this right-angle position with sticky tape.

Try an experimental flight. Make deductions and modifications. Tamper with camber. Sight wings to see if they are on the same plane—and tail fins. Consider weight balance fore and aft, modifying it gently with a spot of tape here and there on the nose or the tail. If you're really excited about it, you will soon be flying.

Captain Barnaby's great paper airplane may seem a difficult challenge to neophytes yet neither it nor any other design is beyond the hopes of any planeophile—a kind of fanatic with patience who, having made a plane and launched it, and having seen it crash, goes back to the drawing board.

BARNABY'S PLANE

Start as before by folding a sheet of 8½-inch by 11-inch paper, but this time folding it crosswise (a). Then open the sheet and fold from one (long) side, starting with ¼ inch fold, and making several folds, increase the width gradually until it comes to ½ inch (b). There should be about 4½ inches

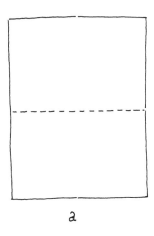

a

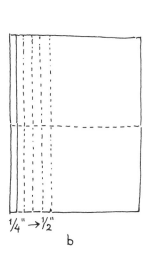

¼" → ½"

b

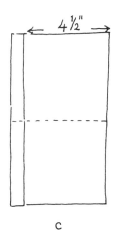

4½"

c

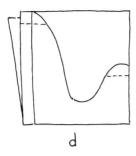

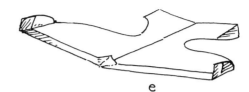

d

e

left unfolded (c). Return paper to original fold and cut wing and tail pattern as illustrated (d). Note stabilizing effect of bending wing tips up and tail fins down. Bend nose up very slightly (e).

GLIDER

Fold an 8½ x 11-inch sheet of paper lengthwise. Fold corners of one end down to meet center fold as in illustration (a). Fold sides down from corners to opposite end of center fold (b). Then fold sides over once more at line where last fold meets side (c). Place small pieces of tape at spots indicated in the illustration (d). The back view of glider should look like illustration (e). Open wings. Bend the tip of the nose down (f).

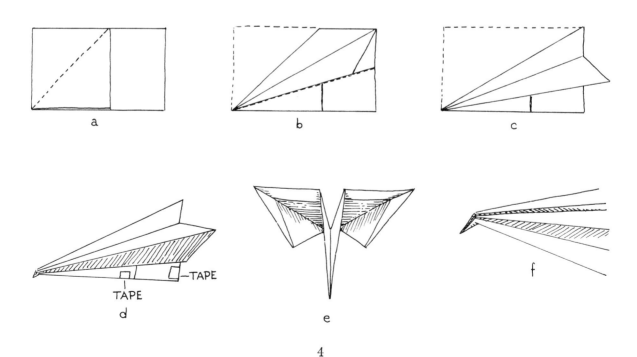

a

b

c

TAPE

TAPE

d

e

f

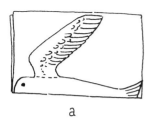
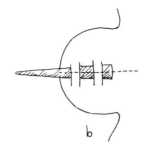

a

b

c

BIRD GLIDER

Take the usual size sheet of paper, though perhaps in a color, and fold it in half crosswise. Follow the illustrated pattern for the wings and tail of the bird (a). Paint on feathers and eyes at this point if you like. Cut slots in the center fold of its neck and head, and run a rolled-up triangle of paper through the slots so that the point of rolled-up paper serves as beak (b). Fold out wings and tail on dotted lines (c).

KITES

Always man has loved the earth and stood on it securely while looking uncertainly into the blue distance, wondering about the sky, dreaming about it and offering it an ethereal kind of love. Our earliest attempts to penetrate this blue dream and learn its secrets may be dated some 2,300 years ago, when Archytas of Tarentum is said to have invented kite-flying (chances are he learned from somebody else). What happened thereabouts doubtless initiated the discovery of the law of aeronautics that led to Benjamin Franklin's experiments with electricity—and then off we go to the airplane, the rocket, and the exploration of outer space.

The original kite was probably very much like the ones we see now—a simple triangle with a semicircular or triangular fore-section. Kites like planes are essentially experimental and the pets of their creators, but generally may be said to involve a cross of rigid members, both tied tightly at the point of crossing, presently covered with paper or other light material.

Kite-flying may have originated in the East. We know that for centuries it has been enormously popular with the Koreans, Chinese, Japanese, Tonkinese, Annamese, Malays, and East Indians. All of these people hold kite-flying festivals, and the Maoris of New Zealand give the occasions an additional artistic touch by buoying up their aircraft with a "kite song."

Of kite stories there are many, such as that of the Korean general of ancient times who sent up a kite with a lighted balloon attached to it, thus making his troops believe that a new star assured them of victory; and the story of another general who used a kite to carry a rope across a gorge as the beginning of building a bridge.

Holidays in time past were often marked by kite festivals, at which contests were held, kite-fighting being the most dramatic. The opponents coat the string near the kite with glue and imbed splinters of glass in it. The "fight" brings out fierce competitive qualities in such amiable men as Will Yolen, world's champion kite flyer. It is not simple combat. The kites must be maneuvered toward each other by men perhaps a hundred yards below, dextrously manipulating their cords, retreating, advancing, suddenly making the thrust. As in all mortal combat, one must fall.

Kiting reached a peak of popularity in nineteenth-century America. Members of the Yorkville United Kite-raising Association in New York City decided that they would send up the biggest kite in history on September 27, 1885. Their craft was 16 feet by 14 feet with a tail 400 feet long. It was covered with cloth that weighed 14 lbs. But patron saint Aeolus failed to smile, and the kite never got up. It was too heavy, and the wind was too light.

When the Columbian Exposition was staged in Chicago in 1893, the Sultan of Johore exhibited fifteen different kinds of kites, these of the Asiatic variety that "bear one or more perforated reeds or bamboos which emit a plaintive sound . . ."

It is said that some people believe that these kites give protection from evil spirits, and leave them up to fly over their houses at night. Such night-flying is a risky business, as I learned in my boyhood, because the wind usually dies away at sundown. One evening, though unworried about evil spirits, I had achieved my greatest kiting success and had teased the hypnotizing triangle almost out of sight. I was reluctant to cancel out my triumph so I hitched the cord to a tree, went to bed, and dreamed peacefully of finding it still there in the morning. It was a dream. There was no kite in the morning, only a limp string that led out of the garden and over neighbors' houses to some remote scene where a kite had crashed in the night. The British usually deliver the incisive comment as in the Encyclopedia Britannica: "usual cause of failure is lack of wind."

As early as the turn of the century, scientists were using kites in many ways, notably in the effort to predict the weather, and to get readings of temperature, humidity, and wind velocity. The military, too, were using them. In 1894 Captain B. F. S. Baden-Powell of the Scots Guards built a kite 36 feet high with which he elevated a man in the interest of observing the terrain for the military. His efforts reached their peak of success when with a system of many kites he lofted a man to the height of 100 feet.

The Encyclopedia Britannica of those days reported, "Roughly speaking, it may be said that each ten square feet of lifting surface on the kite should carry 1,000 feet of 1/32 inch wire without difficulty." Though this report speaks only of kites, one senses in it the thinking of the future— aeronautics and even space travel.

Whether it is the kite or the glider or the plane, the simple dynamics are that a leading edge divides the force of the air so that some goes over a shaped foil and some goes beneath it, the foil being shaped so that the force below slightly exceeds the force above, thus providing lift. Though there are other elements, these are basic, and kite-fliers no doubt had a great deal to do with their discovery.

Benjamin Franklin in 1754 apparently assumed that everybody knew how to make a kite, but he took the trouble to explain how to make one that would, a century and half before the age of electricity, bring this strange violence safely out of the sky. Franklin said:

7

Make a small cross of two light strips of cedar, the arms so long as to stretch the four corners of a large thin silk handkerchief to the extremities of the cross, so you have the body of the kite, which being properly accommodated with a tail, loop, and string, will rise in the air like those made of paper, but this being of silk is fitter to bear the wet and wind of a thundergust without tearing. To the top of the upright stick of the cross is to be fixed a very sharp pointed wire, rising a foot or more above the wood. To the end of the twine, next to the hand, is to be tied a silk ribbon, and where the silk and twine join, a key may be fastened. This kite is to be raised when a thundergust appears to be coming on, and the person who holds the string must stand within a door or window or under some cover, so the silk ribbon may not become wet; and care must be taken that twine does not touch the frame of the door or the window.

Why cedar in particular? Well, you don't question the judgment of a man who was possibly the best kite-flier of the past 3,000 years. One might even wonder if 1754 was not so long ago that in the light of 20th century science Franklin's experiments would appear naive, but the author James Wagonvoord reminds us that, "It was a combination of a Hargrave box kite and Benjamin Franklin's 'antenna' that was flown by Marconi in Nova Scotia when he drew in the first Transatlantic radio signal in 1901."

So men have thus progressed from dreaming about the blue to flirting with it, exploring it, and going beyond it—with kites and planes and rockets.

The secret of flying a kite successfully lies in the original design, its balance and symmetry. Kites are by nature light; early kite-fliers quickly discovered that the larger the kite the more weight it could be expected to lift.

For small kites the lightest materials will serve best: stripped bamboo for the frame, or rattan for round shapes, or very thin straight twigs or the thinnest 3/16-inch dowels. For the frame joints use good white glue, such as Elmer's, and buttonhole cotton thread or fine annealed wire (or split picture wire). All connections should be solid and secure.

Among the best papers to be used for kites are the Japanese rice papers. These come in many types and in many colors. When dry they are strong, but because they collapse when wet, much care must be taken when gluing or painting. It is advisable to use the same glue for the paper as was used for the frame.

The string that goes from your hand to the sky is called kite cord in most sales places, and a 6-lb. strength will give you reasonable flight security anywhere from 500 to 1,000 feet; this is also the usual length of such a ball of string.

A ball of string is awkward to handle unless you have it on a spindle from which you can unroll it easily. Such spindles can be bought and are called

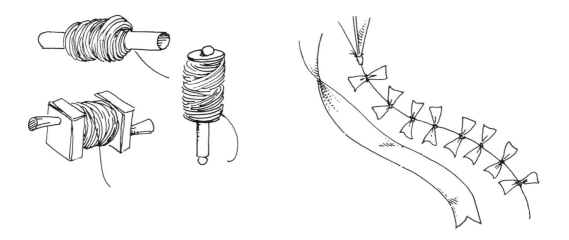

reels, or they will emerge when a roll of Baggies plastic bags has been used up. With a good kite and the string-unrolling problem solved, you just let the line out as your dream ship moves out into the blue.

A kite without a tail is like a man without a wife: usually unbalanced. The tail can be made of kite string with ribbons of crepe paper tied and twisted into them, or just ribbons of crepe paper. The length will be decided by experiment, starting with a short tail such as six feet and lengthening it as instability suggests. So far as possible, use identical pieces of all materials in the tail of the kite, and bring each side in balance with the other.

Of the many kinds of kite design the three described here will help the neophyte get his kite off the ground. They are described as the shield or diamond shape (1), square or rectangular shape (2), and the box shape (3). Each can be made in any size so long as the proportions are adhered to.

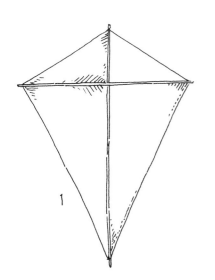

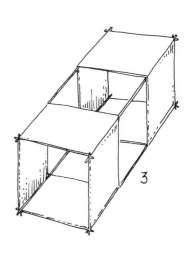

SHIELD OR DIAMOND-SHAPED KITES

Use thinnest dowels or other thin wood sticks, one for the backbone and another for the cross stick (a). Cut a notch on back of main stick and on front of cross stick, the two notches to be brought together and glued and tied securely (b), this junction occurring a quarter of the length from the top of the main stick. As for proportions, the cross stick may be about three-quarters of the length of the main stick.

When glue is thoroughly dry, cut notches ¼ inch from ends of cross stick. Attach string or wire at one end. Bend cross stick slightly and attach wire or string to other end in such a way as to make the cross stick bow (c). Once the wire is tied, put glue on wire and ends to secure. Cut a similar notch at lower end of main stick. Attach a string or wire at end, and at joint of main and cross sticks, which measures the length of the main stick below the joint plus half the length of the cross stick. Here is what is called the belly-band of the kite. Make a small loop knot in belly-band as indicated for the cord that holds the kite in flight (d).

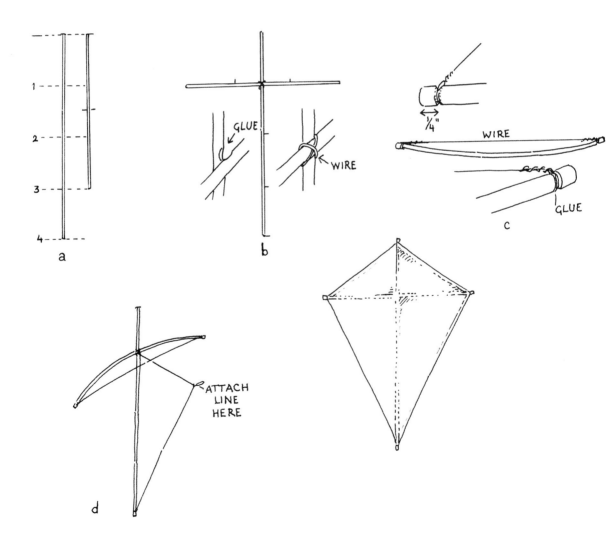

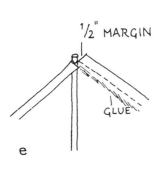

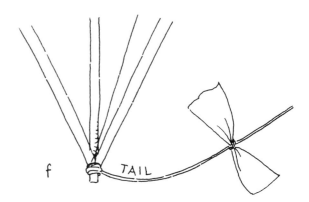

To make the kite you must then cover the wooden cross with paper, putting glue all along the principal members, pressing paper to glue and being careful not to tear the dampened paper. If you wish to use papers of several colors, cut pieces to fit the different sections with a bit extra for the overlap. Overall the paper should be a half inch wider than the frame to provide for the fold on all outside dimensions (e).

Fold over outer margins to inside and glue down. Attach a tail that is two feet or longer, depending on the size of the kite. Hitch to tail-string bows of crepe paper at about 6-inch intervals, these bows being about 3 inches by 5 inches (f). Attach kite line to a loop on your waistband and run into the wind, paying out line. If you have designed well and truly, your kite will head for heaven. If it does not, you should then cut and fit and experiment on the basis of your observation of the kite's behavior.

SQUARE OR RECTANGULAR KITE

Square or rectangular kites derive from Oriental designs, and can be made small or even enormous so long as the proportions are in order. Split bamboo sticks are best for these designs. A good example is a kite that calls for four pieces of bamboo two feet in length, and five pieces 16 inches in length. The shorter ones are cross sticks, the others main sticks. Attach the five cross sticks to the side sticks and the two main sticks (crossed in middle) as in

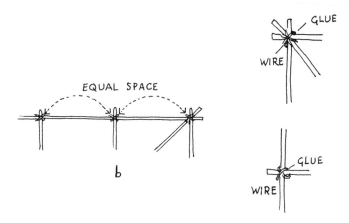

illustration (a). Leave two surplus side pieces for tails. The crossed main sticks must be in back of the cross sticks. Glue all joints and wire them for extra strength (b). Be sure to space cross sticks evenly, and cut the paper with a ½-inch margin on all sides.

Cover frame with paper, put glue on all sticks, and press paper to glue. Fold margin to inside of kite and glue. Attach wire or string to opposite corners of kite, and tighten until main stick forms a slight bow. Tie in this position. Do the same with the other main stick. Make a loop where these ties cross. Attach kite line to loop (c). This kite carries two tails, one on each lower corner, and both tails may carry ribbons of crepe paper.

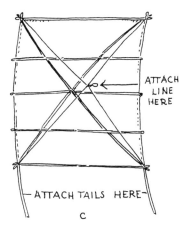

You may wish to paint the kite or decorate it with markers or ink or in any such creative way, this not excluding romantic or humorous comment. Care must be taken to avoid making holes in the paper. If a hole is made, bring the fibers back together by gently pressing paper with your fingertips on a firm, flat surface. Let dry thoroughly.

BOX KITES

Box-shaped kites are of extraordinary interest because aside from Franklin's famous model, they have had more to do with scientific exploration and

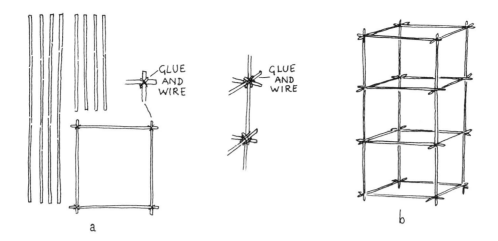

GLUE AND WIRE

GLUE AND WIRE

a

b

discovery than any of the others. They carry a heavy load with great stability and this led scientists to adopt them for the purpose of carrying meteorological instruments into the sky.

To make a box kite, take four split bamboo sticks of equal length, say 18 inches, and sixteen short sticks half that size, 9 inches in this case. Make four squares of the 16 shorter sticks, gluing and wiring all the corners securely (a). Make sure the corners are square. When these squares are completely dry and the glue set, attach the main sticks as illustrated, spacing the squares evenly. Again glue and wire all joints securely, and again let dry thoroughly (b).

Now apply paper. Cut as usual ½-inch wider on each side of two outer sections (c). The paper may be of any color so long as cut to allow for overlap. Fold paper to inside of kite, and glue. This kite needs no tail, and the kite line is attached to only one corner.

Kites of many shapes can be based on these three designs. Using rattan for round-wing shapes, one can make a butterfly kite based on the square kite. Again using rattan, one is free to make circles instead of squares, and produce a tubular kind of kite. Starting off with the shield design, you may send a new star kite off into the sky!

Ours is a wonderful world, and paper-art helps to make it so. On land and sea and in the air, paper art is everywhere. People flying kites, flying planes, shooting off rockets—all must acknowledge their indebtedness to paper-art. A drawing on paper or a folding of paper is where it all began, charting a pathway to the moon, to the other planets, or to the distant stars.

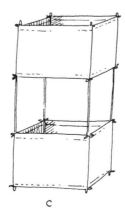

c

BOATS

Sunny afternoons are immortalized in prose, poetry, painting, and all the other arts, partly because they provide a romantic background for budding nautical careers—the sailing of boats by little boys, and their fathers. Witnessing such an idyllic scene, one often wonders whether the sailing of boats is more fascinating to the little boy or the big boy.

This across-the-generations intimacy does not start at the water's edge, but much earlier with the mention of making paper boats. Then it con-

tinues perhaps in the bathroom as one design and another are tried out for seaworthiness. No difference whether the ship is expected to carry a sail or only breast the waves, this is a joint adventure with the collaborators hoping for success.

Whatever the outcome, there is no possibility of failure. Even if the frail vessel should founder and sink, the co-designers will go off hand-in-hand in warm mutuality, determined to design a better ship.

Though for centuries boys of all ages have been making paper boats, there have been new developments in the art. For example, where formerly magnificent paper boats would sail only briefly before becoming waterlogged, now there is a waterproofing liquid available in aerosol spray cans (3M Scotch-guard) which makes such vessels seaworthy and reuseable.

For those wholly innocent of nautical paper art, it will be best to start with simple designs.

FOLDED BOAT

Take an oblong piece of paper with the proportions of four units long to three units wide. Fold it in half as in illustration. Fold it in half again, and open folds out (a). Fold upper corners down to center fold line (b). Mark off some bottom margins and fold them upward and one to each side (c). Overlap ends, then fold them down and bring them together (d). Fold same two ends upward to both sides of point (e). Pull same two ends outward, at the same time pushing point down (f) and pushing fold line inside out (g). Spray with waterproofing from all angles.

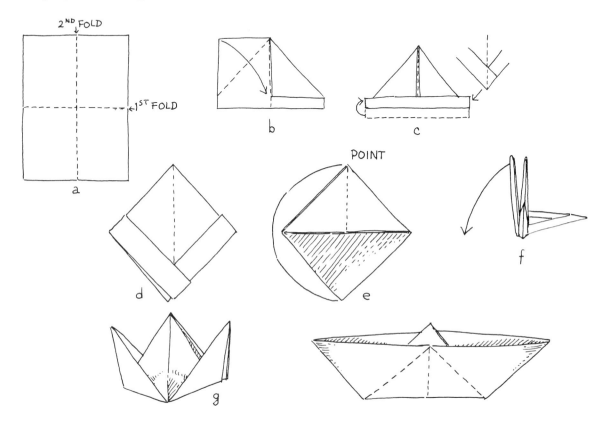

CARDBOARD AND PAPER BOAT WITH SAIL

Make this boat of corrugated cardboard. Cut paper the shape shown in pattern (a). Use a glossy paper or colored bristol (single thickness) or other sturdy foldable paper. Fold in half lengthwise. Cut off corner as indicated (b). Fold stern end over twice, and glue. Fold bow end over three times, and glue. Cut deck line as indicated. Glue in deck section plus or minus ½ inch below deck line. Place glue for mast in bottom of boat about 4¾ inches from stern (c). Glue mast in hole on deck and to bottom of boat. When all the glue is dry, make a sail of bond paper, and attach it to the mast (d). Add a pennant made of double fold of glossy paper. Glue only top edge of pennant so that it can turn freely on mast. Spray the entire boat thoroughly with the waterproof spray.

Before the launching, pour some sand or aquarium pebbles into the hold for ballast, adding or subtracting in accordance with the vessel's ability to carry the sail. Without some ballast the vessel will not sail.

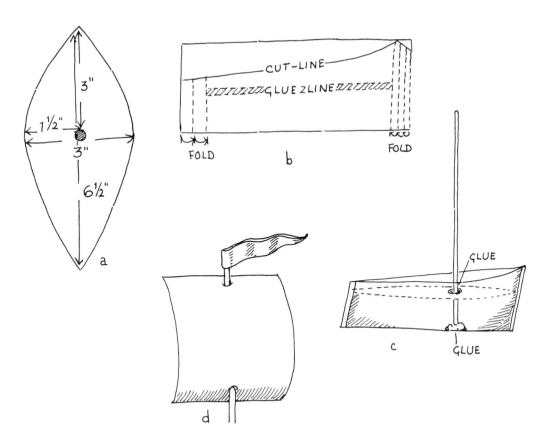

CORRUGATED BOARD BOAT

Cut four pieces of cardboard as in pattern (a). Glue these pieces together. Reinforce with gummed paper tape all around edges (b). The side strip is 1 inch wide and 14 inches long. Cover the entire boat with colored paper or papers of your choice (c). Place the mast as indicated in illustration (d). This mast is made like the one for the cardboard boat above, but 7 inches high. Instead of dousing with champagne, spray liberally with the pressurized waterproofing. Bon voyage!

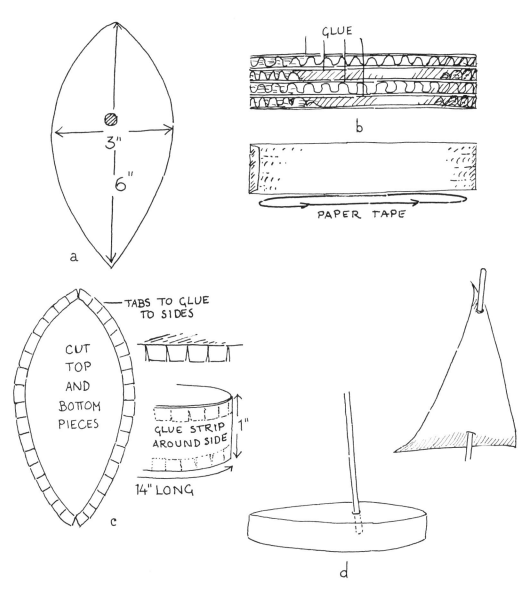

CHAPTER 2

DOLL HOUSES, PLAYHOUSES, FURNITURE AND VILLAGES

Thanks to little girls, doll houses have always been in great demand, and admirers of both are many. The little houses sometimes emerge from humble beginnings like Cinderella, their understructures consisting of boxes, cardboard, paper and cartons—especially movers' cartons because they are larger and stronger. Once they are over-laid with line and color and extravagant decoration, they become dream houses, and several can turn out to be a village.

Playhouses, especially, call for the huge cartons that moving men use because where the doll-house people work from outside, the play-house people are interior decorators; they want cartons large enough so they can get inside with at least a modicum of elbow room.

Secure grocery boxes or cartons that are high enough and wide enough for the design you have in mind. The depth of the box need not be more than 12 inches and if it is deeper than that, cut off some from the front to the right depth with a sharp knife. Consider using a Pepperidge Farm twenty-loaf bread box. This provides for an 18-inch by 20-inch doll house. That is 27 inches to the tip of the gable, and the rooms will be 8 inches deep.

Cut the three flaps of the cover off the box, the remaining flap to be used as a front gable (a). Cut the corners of the gable halfway through, and fold

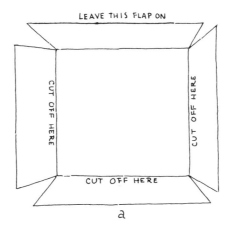

a

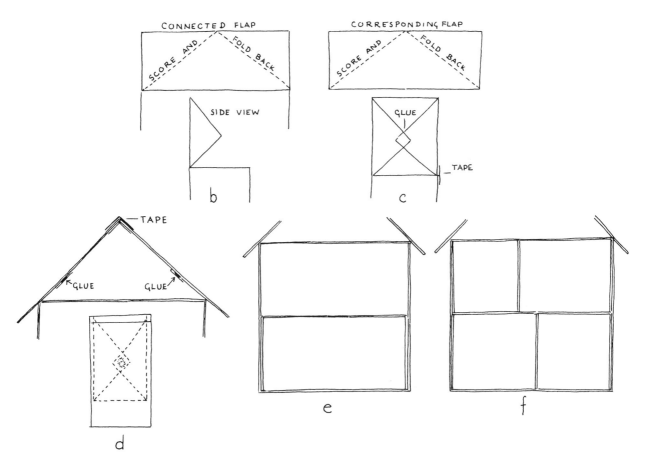

back on the dotted line (b). Cut a similar piece for the back of the house out of the corresponding cut-off piece of the carton cover. With gummed paper tape fasten back gable to back of box. Bend corners back in the same way as with the front (c). Glue corners of front and back together to form support for the roof. Make roof by cutting the two remaining side flaps to a proper size. Avoid having them hang over too far (in this case each piece is 16½ inches by 9 inches.) Use gummed paper tape to connect the two pieces (d).

Now put more glue on the glued-together corners of the gable. Put roof on, centering carefully. Press down on roof until glue sets and holds. With a piece of corrugated board make a division. You could use the separator that comes with the box (e). Now make a partition on each floor, these partitions giving you two rooms on each floor. The partitions are made by cutting a piece of corrugated board to fit the depth and height of the floor (f). Cut two at the same time. If supports on the sides seem advisable, cut two more pieces the same size as the partitions. Some boxes do not have cover flaps wide enough to meet in the middle so that the bottom (now the back) of the box will have an uneven strip down the middle. This can be remedied by leaving a wide enough strip on the back edge of the partition: bend the strip forward, and fit into gap between flaps (g). Reverse the strip on the other partition. This will give you unevenly-sized rooms.

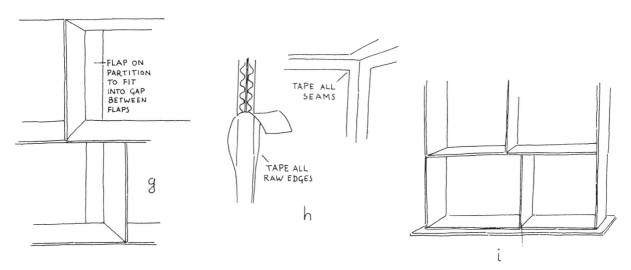

Now everything is ready to be built in. Gummed tape is used throughout. Try to get all corners as square as possible. All seams must be taped to avoid having to contend with hiatuses during the later decoration. Partitions are to be taped on both sides top and bottom, and on both sides to back (h). Tape all raw edges around house. Mount the completed house on a piece of hard corrugated board about one inch larger all around than floor of house, and apply pressure until glue sets, having put plenty of glue between mount and house (i).

When applying gummed tape with a wet sponge, always dampen the board before applying the dampened tape, and then use wet sponge again to dampen the tape on the outside. This will make the tape dry, flat, and taut. When the house is thoroughly taped and thoroughly dry, it is ready to be painted and finished. Use spray paint or poster paint, of course in your own choice of colors. Now is the time to paint on windows and doors if you like.

You may, however, prefer to cover the entire outside with paper. Be sure that all edges are well glued down. A possibility to consider is the pasting on of cut-out windows and doors. If you are ambitious about the effect of windows and doors, it may be best to make them specifically for the particular part of the house where they will be before the "taping together." Make doors by cutting height and width of door. Score the other side halfway through the board. Tape this side (the hinges) with Mystik tape on both sides. Do not, of course, tape bottom edge of door when taping partition (j).

If you wish shutters on the windows then make them the same way. Otherwise just cut out square or oblong windows, tape the edges, and finish off when decorating. If you want more elaborate windows, cut frame of thin cardboard (such as the laundry puts in men's shirts) and use cellophane or plastic wrap for window panes. Cover all raw edges with gummed tape.

Avoid using cracked or otherwise damaged corrugated board or boxes because it is nearly impossible to cover the blemishes unless you use bristol board and similar papers for covering.

Methods of decoration are as limitless with doll houses as with any other kind of house because this is one of the ways in which individual artistry and taste are expressed. Gift-wrap papers constitute a rich source for doll-house wallpaper. Some such papers are suitable for the floors. It is possible to make marvelous paintings to hang on the walls, using wildlife stamps or reproductions of paintings found in magazines. Details of how to make these and other furnishings will be found in the doll house-furnishing section of this chapter.

PORTABLE DOLL HOUSES

A special kind of doll house is one that can be taken along on trips and set up where perhaps only a little floor space is available. It is easy to make, and folds up and packs as easily as a book.

Cut out of 2-ply cardboard eight equal squares. You can make them any size you wish. Ten inches is a convenient size (a). Use a sharp knife in cutting the squares out of hard 2-ply cardboard ⅛ inch thick.

Use Mystik tape 1¼ inches wide for taping. Tape edges of two squares together on one side (b). Fold the squares together, and tape the same two edges together on the opposite side. Do the same taping with the other three pairs of squares.

The next step is to attach all four double pieces to each other in the middle so that you have four attached walls of four rooms (c). The floors are already attached to the walls. Do not attach the floors in any other way to anything, leaving them free to be folded up to the walls for closing.

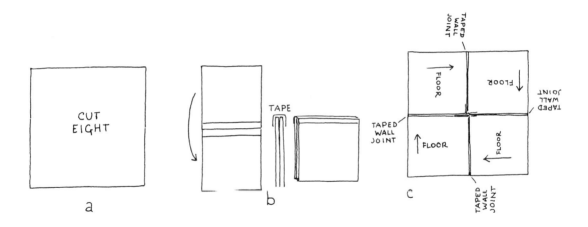

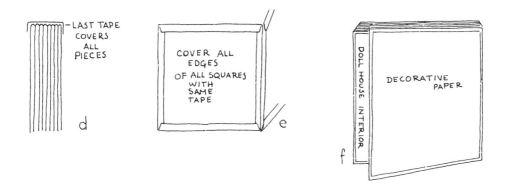

Tape the four walls together in the middle as with the other pieces. Do, however, leave a little more space between the edges of squares. Tape only one side each time. Now fold the whole house to be sure it works. First, fold floor to walls, and close the four double pieces as you would a book (d). The last tape goes on across the backs of all four double pieces. Finish all raw edges with the same tape (e). Cover floor backs with fancy paper such as gift wrap (f).

Decorate walls and floors with your choice of papers. In decorating the eight walls, make cut-out furnishings to paste on or paint some furnishings directly on the paper. Other furnishings can be made as described in this chapter. A special container should be made for carrying them when the house is folded.

If you want to you can make one of the four areas seem to be outside the house. Paint the floor to look like a yard. Either paint walls or use cut-out windows and doors on walls. You can paste cut-out gardens on walls, too, using colorful pictures from garden magazines and seed catalogs.

PLAYHOUSES

Packing boxes, the bigger the better, make very good playhouses. Cats and children discovered this long before their patrons and elders, usually after a move to a new house. Once the packing boxes are emptied and sitting around, the children move into them, seeing them as make-believe houses, castles or fortresses, or even cathedrals—whatever their imagination suggests. Apprised of this charming childish interest in boxes, one or another of the moving companies has printed windows and doors on their boxes so that with a little cutting, instant playhouses are made. Of course they must be decorated further.

Yet with paper and paint and glue and strong staples, a marvelous house can be made out of a packing carton, even a whole street of shops and houses. Here everything is large scale, since children will be getting in and out of the houses—the cut-out doors large, and the decorations bold.

The suggestions are intended to point the way for individual imagination, and supported by such imagination the avenues may sparkle with boutiques and shops and theatres—and whatever else! Would not a puppet theatre seem very likely?

To make the house, cut out windows and doors, score hinge side and tape hinges with Mystik tape (a). Put on a roof made of two pieces of hard corrugated board. Cut off corners of top of box (b). No gluing is needed.

For a soda shop or drugstore, a soda fountain is required. In designing such a structure, plan for a large cut-out window in front and a door in back (c). This and any other stores can best be made of the 2-piece roof building. Cut door in the back. Flap down the counter to the outside as in the illustration and make support of counter as shown. Equip the soda fountain with stools of a toadstool design.

For the puppet theater, consider making one large window, folding the lower edge inward (d). Cut proscenium arch of hard corrugated cardboard, and glue to front of the stage.

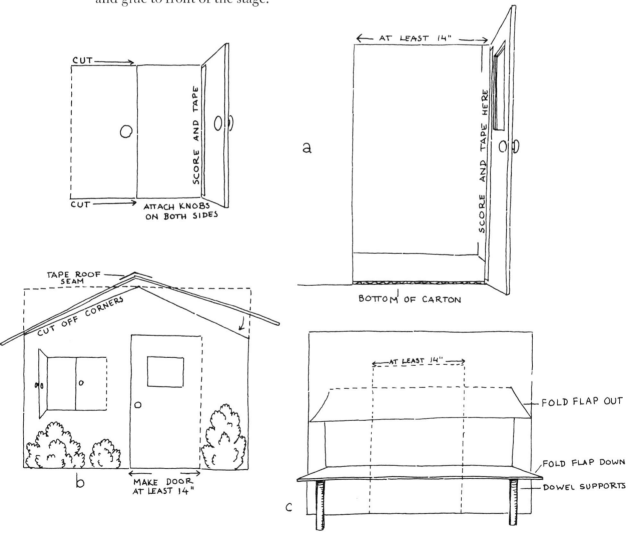

TAPE ROOF
SEAM

FOLD THIS EDGE
INWARD

SET THEATRE ON
TABLE TOP

d

OTHER PLAYHOUSES

Playhouses may be made from scratch from corrugated board, and this calls for considerable artistry and construction ability. In terms of the construction problem, attention should be directed to the support structure. The size of the building may be governed by the size of the sheets of board available.

In making the houses out of large sheets of corrugated board, use two pieces for two walls, and divide another piece for the other two walls. Tape all the seams with reinforced gummed paper packing tape. Tape the outside of the folding edge (a). Make the roof of four equal pieces (b). Rest roof on top of walls. Cut doors in front and back of house (c).

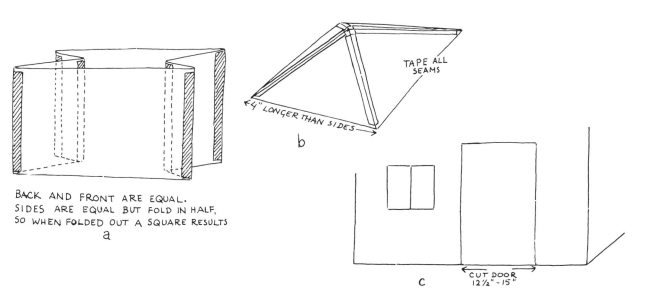

TAPE ALL
SEAMS

4" LONGER THAN SIDES

b

BACK AND FRONT ARE EQUAL.
SIDES ARE EQUAL BUT FOLD IN HALF,
SO WHEN FOLDED OUT A SQUARE RESULTS

a

CUT DOOR
12½" - 15"

c

CHILDREN'S FURNITURE

The bench is an important part of children's furniture. A good base is the kind of carton that heavy bottles come in, especially wine or spirits, because they are strongly made to protect the fragile glass and the valuable contents. Many such cartons are designed to support 200 lbs. per square inch. Most liquor stores will give you a few cartons, and hopefully still containing the bottle separators because these strengthen the carton like the inner members of a building; this strength is greatest in the cartons designed for pint bottles. Some grocery store cartons are similar, but they seldom are as well constructed or have as many separators.

Whatever the basic structure, examine carefully for basic strength, and fit any torn or cut pieces together, and repair them with glue, reinforcing by applying gummed tape to the damaged areas and over the raw edges.

Now you can transform the humble box into a wonderful bench by covering it with boldly printed paper or paper of an interesting solid color. To accomplish this you place the box in the center of the paper of your choice, having previously determined that it is large enough to cover the top and sides of box plus runover. Cut as in pattern (a). Glue longest sides against sides of box. Glue down the run-over area and side flaps. Then glue down

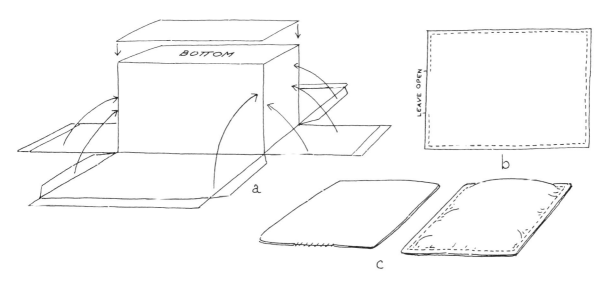

other side pieces and their run-over. Cover bottom with paper from edge to edge. Trim off edges carefully. Make a pillow for the bench out of paper cloth or crepe paper.

To make the pillow, cut two pieces of fabric slightly larger than the top of the bench (about one inch surplus all around). With the right sides together, sew seams three-quarters of an inch from edge of fabric (b). Leave three inches at one end open (for stuffing later). Turn inside out, and stuff with the fluffiest kind of stuffing you have, such as foam rubber or cheese-cloth. Sew last three inches by hand with an overhand stitch. Now sew a line of stitching all around the pillow at about one-half-inch from the edge. Use any stitch you prefer, perhaps a chain stitch or a machine stitch (c).

For the toadstool kind of stool, you start by cutting a strip of single-faced corrugated cardboard about ten inches wide, cut squarely and true. The length of the strip should be five feet. Then from another piece of corrugated board, cut two strips 10 inches by 3 inches, cutting the pieces with the corrugations running lengthwise. Cut one slot in each piece as indicated, and push them together (a). Put glue all along the four seams, and let dry thoroughly. Try to keep the pieces at right angles until the glue dries thoroughly. Glue one end of the long strip to one side of the cross piece, and roll the entire strip around cross piece until used up. Secure edge with glue, and then apply 10-inch strip of gummed paper to seam. This is the stem part of the toadstool (b).

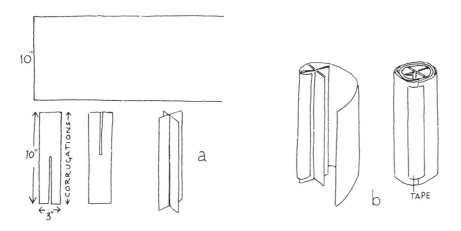

To make the seat, you draw four ten-inch circles on hard double-faced corrugated board, then cut them out with a sharp knife or single-edge razor blade, and glue them together back to back, alternating the directions of the corrugations. This makes a very solid seat. All raw edges should be covered with gummed paper tape (c).

The fastening of seat to stem involves putting the seat upsidedown on a level surface so that with center stem on seat, its outline can be drawn. (Usually the stem is not exactly round.)

Now put a generous amount of glue on seat bottom within the outline of stem. Place the stem back on seat, matching its outline, and press tightly together, holding for a bit to get matching surfaces aligned. Make sure there is plenty of glue all around stem connection. Let dry completely (d). Make four equal 8½ inch circles for foot. Combine them in exactly the same way as the construction of the seat, and attach the foot to the other end of the stem, then giving care to the drying process (e).

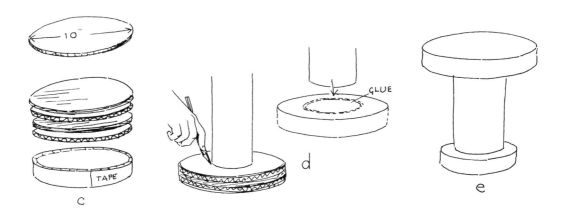

Cover each toadstool with white paper except for the seat which deserves red paper. Cut two ten-inch circles (plus one-half inch for tabs). Glue one to top of seat, gluing tabs down to side of seat. Draw outline of stem on second circle, cut one-half inch within that outline, cut tabs, and through resulting ring (f) glue to bottom of seat. Cover the foot the same way as the seat. Cover the stem last, using a 10-inch-wide strip of paper. The length needed will vary, and may be determined by measuring the circumference of the stem with cloth measuring tape.

For a round full pillow for the seat of a toadstool, start with red paper cloth or any such fabric. Cut a circle of the size of the seat, plus ¾-inch for the seam. Cut another circle about 1½ inch larger than the seat, plus ¾-inch

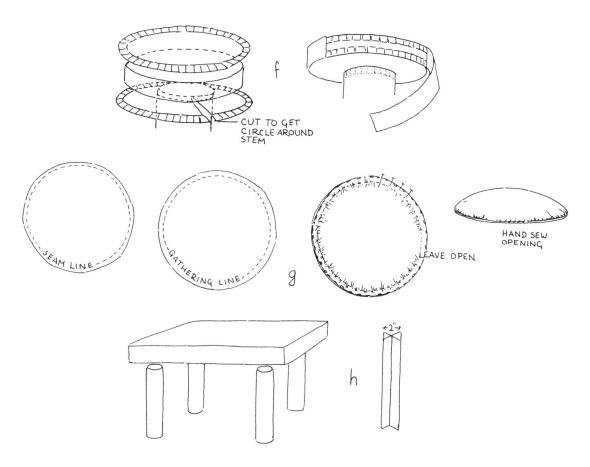

for the seam. Gather whole seamline of larger circle and pin to smaller circle, spacing evenly all around. Sew seam leaving 3-inch opening for stuffing. Turn inside out, and fill with semi-soft stuffing. Hand sew the last three inches of seam (g).

The table inevitably follows the stool, and is made in much the same way as the stool. Make the tabletop rectangular or round. Make four legs in the same way you would make the stem of the stool (h). However, make each cross piece only 2 inches wide and 15 inches high. Roll a few layers of single-faced corrugated board around legs. Attach in the same way to table top as the stem of the stool was attached to the seat. Finish and cover in the same way, too. Be sure to make all four legs exactly equal in length so that the table will not wobble.

DOLL HOUSE FURNITURE

Small furniture is wonderfully interesting, and for making it matchboxes are very useful, especially the small ones. Take one large match box and four small ones. Use the inside of the large box for a sofa. Cut a piece out of the side of the large box to accommodate the arm rest. Make a similar cut on the other side (a). Cover the seat of the large box with any paper that would

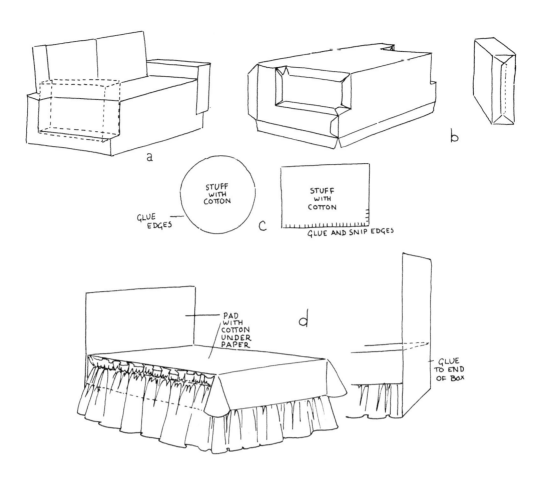

look like upholstery. Follow illustrations for sides. Cover backrests and arm-rests with the same paper, and then glue them in place (b). Make a few tiny pillows of crepe paper stuffed with cotton (c).

For a bed, use cover of large match box which lends itself to decoration with many papers that look like bedding (crepe paper being the easiest and the best because it can be ruffled). Cover open ends with tape or paper. Then make a head rest for the bed by cutting a piece of cardboard in a shape of your choice but one that will fit head-end of bed (d). Cover with appropriate paper, and glue to the head of the bed.

For a chest of drawers, assemble three of the small match boxes to construct a small cabinet, or three of the large size for a sizable chest. Stack box covers with glue in between. Cover seams and edges with gummed paper tape. Decorate stack by covering with fancy paper or plain colored paper. Glue on beads for handles, or insert envelope clips. Make feet of envelope clips. Cover back with plain paper before finishing with fancy paper.

A table can be made of a piece of heavy cardboard cut to any interesting shape. Make holes halfway through the board, using an awl or a screw (e).

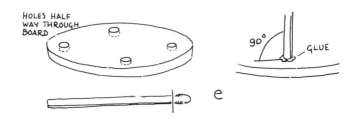

Snip off the heads of four wooden matches (or three) with a pair of pliers, taking care to make the sticks the same length. Inject glue into each hole, and insert matches at right angles to the top. Let dry this way. If necessary support the matches to insure that they will dry at right angles to the top. Cover the table with appropriate paper.

Cabinets are a necessary and artistic part of home decoration. To create one use any suitable small box. Make doors by cutting as on dotted lines in illustration (f). The hinges require a little scoring to be flexible enough. Care must be taken not to score too deeply lest the doors come off. For really workable doors, score nearly through the board, then apply a strip of Mystik tape on the seam. When the cabinet has been covered with paper (cover doors separately) attach beads to the doors with glue as handles or use envelope clips (g).

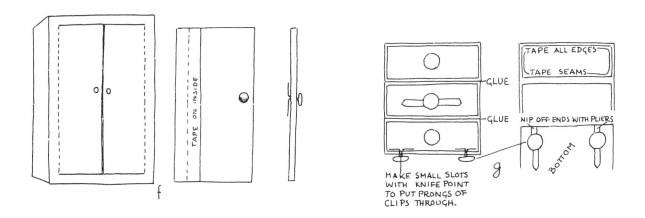

A room must have chairs, and chairs may be made of thin cardboard, as in pattern (h). Fold the legs down along the dotted lines and fold the back up on the dotted line. Glue front leg seams as shown in the illustration. Cover the seat with bright paper. Perhaps artists will wish to paint the rest of the chair.

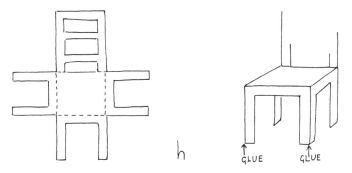

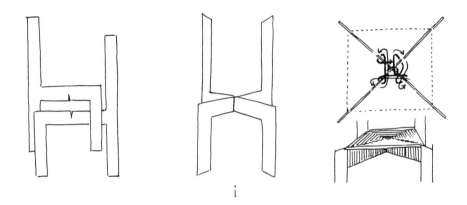

i

Another kind of chair will call for thin string (or possibly raffia if larger chairs are made). Cut two pieces of cardboard as in pattern (i). Fit pieces together in the middle. Weave seat with string as indicated.

Flowers are essential to any household decoration and this special art will be dealt with in Chapter 6.

Of course such an elegant house will have pictures, and these are ready to hand. Postage stamps and wild life stamps reproduce beautiful paintings of stern patriots, architecture, and flora and fauna. The magazine illustrations provide art perhaps equally interesting.

To frame, cut pieces of cardboard slightly larger than the picture to be framed. Stick picture down, centering it carefully and leaving an even margin all around (j). Use embossed gold strip to make the frame, gluing down the edging so that no loose ends remain. Mitre the corners, cutting at a 45-degree angle.

A house must have mirrors, for which you will do best to use heavy aluminum foil, which is better than the ordinary kitchen variety. Glue a piece of foil onto a piece of cardboard that is slightly larger (k). Now frame the mirrors as you previously framed the pictures.

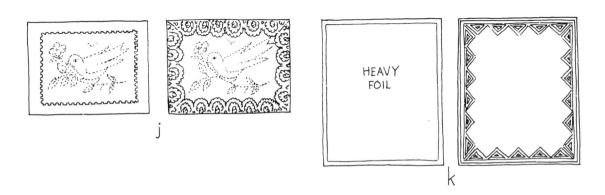

j

HEAVY FOIL

k

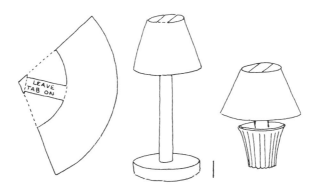

So far the house has been dark, and can only be lighted by lamps. One way to dispel the darkness is to make a standing lamp. Make a lampshade from a piece of paper rolled as a circular cone, leaving a tab for support as shown in pattern (1). Place the shade atop a thin piece of dowel, and place dowel in a base made of 3-ply cardboard, roughly the diameter of the lampshade. Make table lamps in a similar way using small containers or tube caps for bases.

VILLAGES

Villages can be made out of paper, and the unit of the village is the house. Use poster board throughout, or durable weight bristol board. In planning the sizes and arrangement of your windows and doors, you may find inspira-

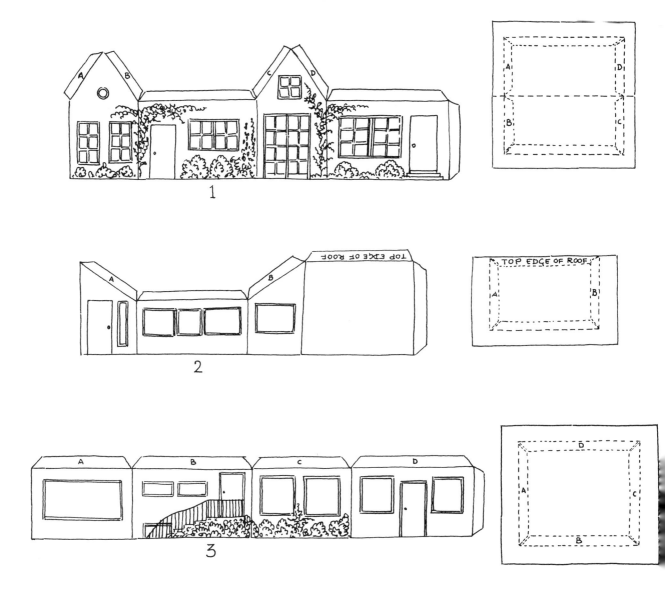

tion in magazine photos. In general follow the design for the three types of houses shown (1, 2, 3). These can be varied by varying their exterior decoration. Glue tabs to parts of buildings as indicated.

Besides windows and doors, decorate each building with some foundation plantings. This can be done by sticking on cut-outs or by painting them on with poster paint or the wick-markers.

Fairly large houses can be made using cartons from the grocery or liquor stores. The same method is used in either case, though with the stauncher cartons no wall sections are needed. The roof can be added with no other support than the tabs. The gables are made the same as for the doll house described at the beginning of this chapter (4).

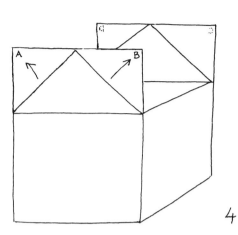 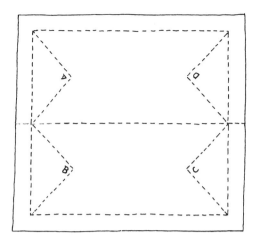

4

The center of the village may well be the church. This is made much like the houses. Make the steeple either in one piece with a tower section made of a cone (5). Snip lower edge of cone, and glue it to square top of tower. If carton-houses are used for the village, add a proportionately larger tower to your church, made of course of corrugated board.

5

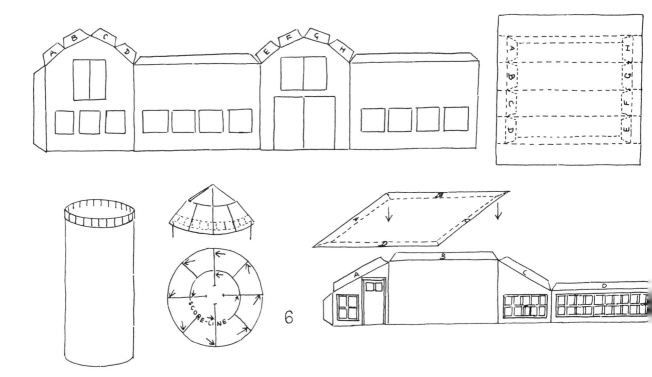

A village is likely to have an outlying farm or two, and so perhaps could include a farmhouse with a few lean-to structures. The barn is made in a way similar to the church, the silo corresponding to the tower. The silo is a cylinder with a cone roof (6).

Construct the stores the same way as the houses, adding here and there a lean-to to the fronts (7). With all these buildings—and the creator's personal imagination—and trees and patches of green paper for grass areas (Swiss velour) a little world appears.

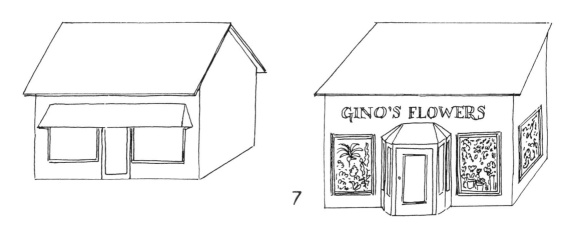

CHAPTER 3

LANTERNS, LAMPSHADES AND WINDOW PICTURES

People of town and country share many attitudes and attributes, and here special notice is taken of those who have taste and artistic instincts. Wherever they live, these special people will find excitement in creating their own individual lanterns, lampshades, and window pictures because here originality has free rein and of course because they want their houses to be their very own—different from anybody else's.

How better could you make your castle unique than by having a lampshade of your creation at the entrance, lampshades inside that are originals because you made them, and perhaps lanterns of your design on the terrace or in the garden?

What of the window picture, that almost forgotten Victorian artistic delicacy, given here a phoenix-like reappearance? When windows look out on beautiful surroundings, a window picture seems like a splendid jewel in a beautiful setting. When, sadly, the view is not beautiful, as in cramped city surroundings, the window picture creates the illusion of a beautiful view.

Especially for those city-dwellers who live mostly indoors, the designing and making of their own lampshades will assume a special importance. For their gardens they may wish to extend their creativity to lanterns offering a wide latitude of expression.

Then there are window pictures and shadow effects related to all of the foregoing, as well as lanterns designed for religious, pagan, and other celebrations of an indeterminate nature. For example:

LANTERN WITH VOTIVE LIGHT

To make a lantern with a votive light, provide yourself with a dark-colored poster board, green or brown, and any thin translucent paper in colors you may wish to use as backing for the figures in each frame. Use a sharp knife to cut out your decorations.

Draw your decorations and the framework for the back of the lantern on the back of the board. Cut out all the parts that you wish to show light (a).

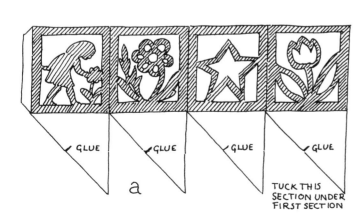

GLUE   GLUE   GLUE   GLUE

a

TUCK THIS
SECTION UNDER
FIRST SECTION

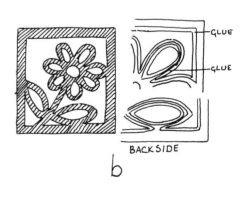

GLUE

GLUE

BACKSIDE

b

38

Be sure to leave connections between figures and frame. Glue the thin colored paper to back side of figures. Give each piece of paper a large enough margin to overlap onto the board. Trim excess (b). Glue frame together at side tab. Fold diagonal sections over each other, and hook each piece to the next at the notches. For extra strength put a little glue between all the pieces. Measure the size of resulting bottom, and cut a piece of heavy aluminum foil to fit inside. Cut a similar piece of foil, cut a star in the center and bend the points up (c). This is the holder for the votive light. Now attach four wires of equal length through the corners of the lantern. Bring the wires together (d) and twist into a hook for hanging.

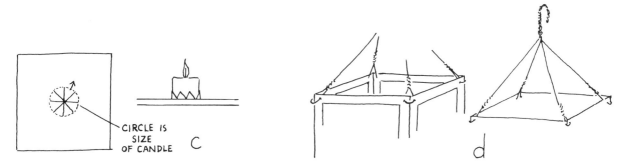

CHINESE LANTERNS

Rattan or cotton-covered wires are suitable for making the rings needed in the framework of this lantern. Make one ring for each end, and at least two more for in-between. Cut equal pieces (as many as you decide to use). Bring ends together to form circles. Splice ends of rattan or twist ends of wire (a). Measure a piece of tissue paper or kite paper about ¼ inch wider on both sides than height of lantern. Measure and draw lines on wrong side of paper (b). Paper should be long enough to equal the circumference plus overlap of ½ inch. Put glue on circle. Starting at one end roll the

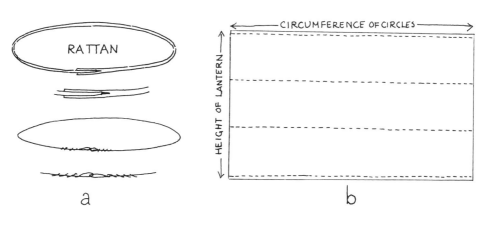

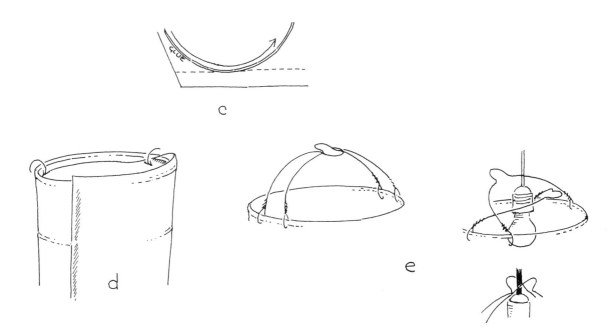

c

d

e

circle towards the other end following penciled line (c). When all rings have been glued to the paper, finish the lantern by turning margins at both ends to inside, and gluing them. Trim the side seam if necessary, and glue the overlap (d).

A hanger may be made by attaching two half circles of wire to upper edge of lantern. Make a half loop in each wire (e) to place over light fixture, folding wires back crosswise. Release lantern and wires. (They will fit around cord above fixture.)

CHRISTMAS LANTERNS WITHOUT LIGHTS

These are lantern-shaped ornaments for use as Christmas tree decorations and for supplementary use with mobiles. Cut a strip of bright paper. This should have 3x5 proportions for short stocky lanterns (a), 3x4 for longer slimmer ones (b), and 5x4 for the double one (c).

For first two lanterns, fold the paper in half lengthwise, and clip on dotted lines. Fold open and staple or glue the overlapping ends, top and bottom (a and b). For the double lantern, fold strip on line 2. Clip on dotted lines. Fold strip on line 3, and unfold cut piece. Staple or glue the overlapping ends, top and bottom (c).

Imaginative people will make these lanterns of many shapes and sizes and of many bright and beautiful colors. Staple several to ribbons to use as garlands.

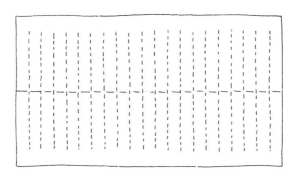

a

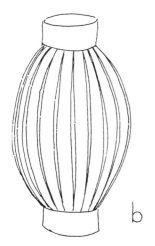

b

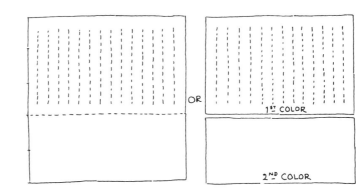

c

OR

1ˢᵗ COLOR

2ᴺᴰ COLOR

Pleated lamp shades are the easiest to make. They are also the most versatile because they can be fitted to almost any lamp without significant change in structure. You make a shade for wall lights with pleats running up and down (7) or a cone-shaped shade (2) or a cylindrical shade (3). Though producing different effects, they are basically the same. (To avoid any fire hazard, always leave a chimney or vent of some kind over the light bulbs, and be careful to avoid letting any light bulb come too close to your shades.)

1

2

3

One of the most difficult details is finding the right wire base to rest the shade on. Almost all lamps have a different structure, so one has to find the wire shade base that will fit the lamp. Often the best solution is to use old shade bases.

There are many ways to pleat a shade. All the pleat-lines should be scored (see page xiii) to break the paper surface just enough to make folding easy and neat without cracks.

There are many papers suitable for pleating shades. It will be best to find paper that is crisp and thick enough to hold its shape without having to recrease or fold it. Many drawing papers such as lightweight bristol, lightweight aquarel paper, or vellum, are suitable because they have a translucent quality. Colored papers may be used though they are usually not as translucent, and the colors do not always benefit by back-lighting. There is a paper called Japanese lace paper which makes a beautiful shade, when backed by tissue paper or a stronger paper such as thin vellum. (See page 42). This is done before pleating, and takes quite a bit of careful handling.

To start, measure a piece of paper as wide as the height of the shade, and as long as six times the diameter of the widest part of the shade. Mark and score the paper on the wrong side, and mark everything very lightly with pencil; if you use pencil very carefully, no erasing will be needed.

To get a straight edge at the bottom and a pleated edge at the top, measure paper only to the circumference (a cloth tape measure) or the widest edge, plus as always a ½ inch overlap for closing shade.

Most sheets of paper are not large enough for a good-sized shade, so that you will have to piece a few strips together. Use white glue for this purpose. Mark paper at regular intervals (½-inch or ¾-inch) along both edges (a). Score at corresponding marks, and then fold the paper on score lines. Alternate folds inward and outward (b). Punch holes along dotted line about three-quarters of an inch from edge of inside pleats, cutting edge each time (c). Resulting little hooks will fit over wire of the lampshade's base. For extra

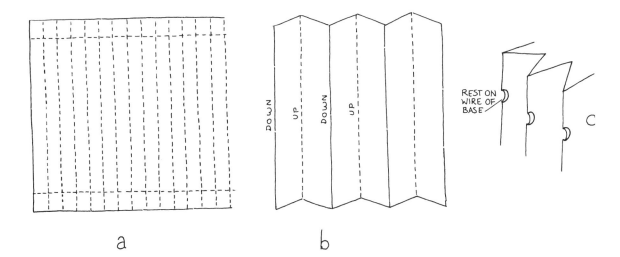

a   b

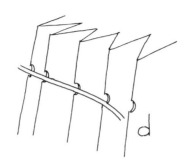

security cut small notches in the outside pleat edges. Tie a string or cord around the shade, passing the string over all the notches (d). Tie a knot and cut off loose ends. (For a few other ways to pleat: follow the various patterns, scoring every line on the back of the paper.)

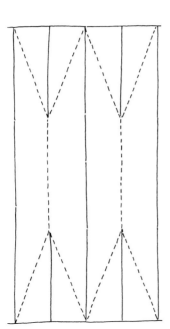
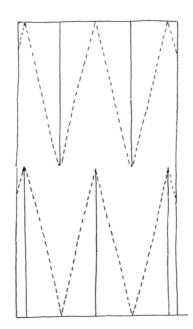
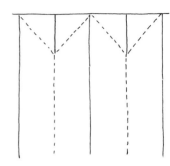

MERRY-GO-ROUND LAMPSHADE

All lampshades because of their special dimensions of light, color, and late-day associations are *prima-facie* romantic, and in a lampshade that *moves* we see an extra dimension.

Such extra-dimensional lampshades may be made as here described. Start with a cylindrical shade made of any vellum or bristol board. Preferably

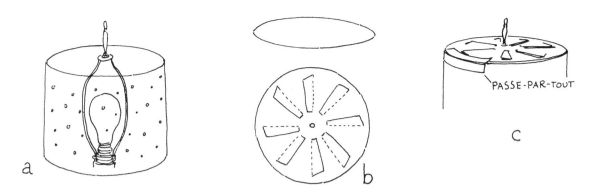

a

b

PASSE-PAR-TOUT

c

use a lyre lamp fixture (a). Punch according to your artistic pleasure tiny holes in the paper before you close the cylinder. Your artistic fancy can run riot in designing the hole-patterns, random or paisley or whatever, visualizing withal the spots of light coming through.

Lights are interesting, and colored lights may be more interesting. For this make large holes in the cylinder, and back them up with one or more colors of tissue paper, or cut merry-go-round figures out of opaque paper, and glue them to the inside of the shade. The measurement for the top (same paper as the shade) will be of the same dimensions. In this disc cut radial gashes as in illustration (b). Bend triangular pieces up to serve as vents for the heat coming up from the lamp bulbs. Make a hole in the exact center to fit easily around pin of the lamp fixture. Glue circle to shade, and cover the seam with paper passe-partout. Place the shade over the pin of fixture, turn on the lamp, and the heat of the bulb will start the shade turning (c).

THE CUT-OUT SHADE

In creating the illustration, dogwood was used. Any other flower, fruit, or leaves may provide a pleasing design. Start by measuring the wire frame to be used for the shade. Then cut a piece of paper to correspond out of vellum or other paper stiff enough to hold its shape. On the inside or wrong side of paper draw the design lightly with pencil (a) and with a sharp whittling knife or razor (X-Acto) cut through paper along pencil lines, always leaving a connecting piece of line, or ladder, uncut. Prick holes with awl for flower centers. Score a few other details. Then very carefully bend the leaves and flowers outward—about 1/16-inch, as shown in illustration (b). The light of the lamp will shine through the design, giving a three-dimensional effect.

PRICK HOLES

SCORE

CUT

VICTORIAN WINDOW PICTURES

You can make delightful rosette windows with four colors of tissue paper. Fold each piece as in cutting doilies.(See page 133). Start with squares of equal size. Fold each square in half, in half again, and then twice diagonally (a).

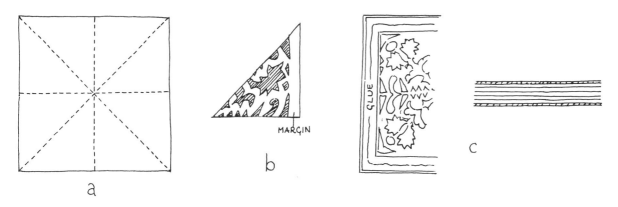

a

b

MARGIN

GLUE

c

Leave on points, always leaving a ½-inch margin as part of the design for the frame (b). Cut an intricate design (sketch the design first if it gives you greater confidence).

Cut a different design in each sheet of tissue paper. Measure two square frames of cardboard (coated, or cover later) with inside measurements the same as the inside measurements of the margins of the tissues. Glue margins of tissue squares between the frame, one on top of the other, centers and corners meeting, being careful to even out corners (c).

Hang picture in window by one of the corners or lean it against the window. The flow of color is reminiscent of that in cathedrals. In making a small rosette with a fine and delicate design, nail or cuticle scissors will be helpful. For a large rosette it is important to use strong cardboard for the frame, and because the large tissues are difficult to use, they must be handled delicately.

FLOWERS IN STAINED GLASS

Draw a design on black or other dark-colored board. With a sharp knife (X-Acto or Frisket) cut out the part of the design that will let light through the tissues (a). The remaining cardboard will be the frame. Now cut out pieces of tissue paper or other translucent paper to the size of the open part of the design, plus a very narrow margin for gluing (b). Use as many colors

a

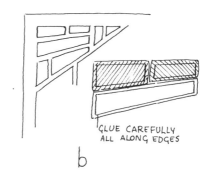

GLUE CAREFULLY
ALL ALONG EDGES

b

as you think will create a dazzling effect. Be careful not to over-run margins. Cover the back of the design with very thin white paper to produce a finished look.

Crowning all these endeavors, place your window picture or hang by a string or fine wire from the window frame. If one is worth making, it is worthwhile to make several, and several might be combined as a mobile, in which case paint margins on the back side black or the color of the front and forget about backing with white paper.

NIGHTSCAPE

Draw a house surrounded by a few trees on a piece of dark board. Cut out a few windows and a window in the door. Also cut out the sky (a). Leave a margin all around for a frame. Glue a piece of yellow tissue paper behind the house. Glue a piece of dark blue paper against back for the sky. Prick holes in sky for stars, and cut out a sickle moon (b). Hold it up against the light, and you are looking at a nightscape.

Here, as everywhere else in paper-art, you are dealing with your own aesthetic resources, and you may be surprised to find them greater than you thought.

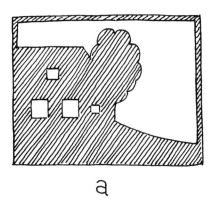

a

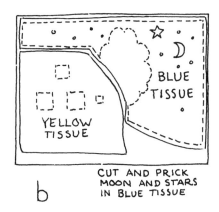

YELLOW TISSUE

BLUE TISSUE

b

CUT AND PRICK MOON AND STARS IN BLUE TISSUE

CHAPTER 4

APRONS, COSTUMES
AND MASKS

Dressing gaily can brighten every day for a woman, and also for a little girl: so young for the grownup, and so grownup for the young. What excitement for the men and boys!

Fun for all concerned, paper-art opens up new vistas for making things: dresses, aprons, costumes, and masks for party time, colorful dresses and aprons for any time. Important to our fair ladies, when you go to a party wearing a dress or a costume you have made yourself, you know for sure that you will not meet someone else wearing the same model.

APRONS

Especially good for parties are creatively colorful aprons. Of course, they are made for the excitement of a special occasion, and not expected to last for more than a party or two. They may be made by the simplest pattern with only a few seams to sew. The design should be of the kind that will give freedom of movement without putting a strain on any part of the garment. When sewing by machine, use the largest stitch size—about ⅛ inch.

Every fashion pattern book has several suggestions for aprons that are simple to make. Here are several ideas that are specific enough and yet give wide latitude to the designer's talents. Start out with the idea of making the aprons of white crepe paper sprayed with Scotch-guard so that spillage will spoil neither the apron nor the clothing underneath.

Start to make an apron by measuring the waist. Then cut a strip of crepe paper as long as the waist measurement, plus enough to tie a bow. This strip should be about 3 inches wide or a bit more if you want a wider waistband. For a stronger waistband, sew a 1½-inch gauze bandage into the waistband.

Now cut a piece of crepe paper to the length you want, and cut with the grain running up and down. Of the different widths of crepe paper, the 20-inch width may be most suitable. Gather ¾ inch from the top (on dotted line) (a). Baste with large stitches the center back of the waistband to the

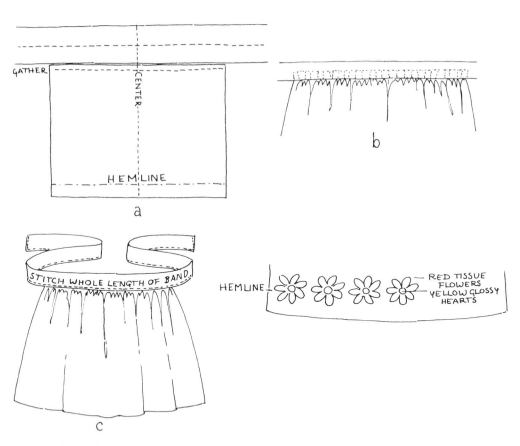

a

b

STITCH WHOLE LENGTH OF BAND.

c

HEMLINE — RED TISSUE FLOWERS — YELLOW GLOSSY HEARTS

center of the skirt. Sew only the part connected with the skirt (b). Fold waist-band over to the front and pin there.

To stitch the waistband, start at one end and run through the entire length. Turn up the hem, and fasten with transparent tape. The hem is not essential, but it gives the apron a finished look. You may give free rein to your artistic instincts by snipping cut-outs of any kind and color, such as colored tissue-paper flowers with glossy-paper hearts. Paste on with a mini-mum of glue. The apron might well be sprayed with Scotch-Guard before adding the decorations.

OTHER APRONS

For another apron cut a circle of crepe paper, and cut off a segment for the waistline (a). Cut a strip a few inches wide that is six times the diameter

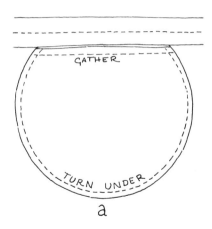

GATHER

TURN UNDER

a

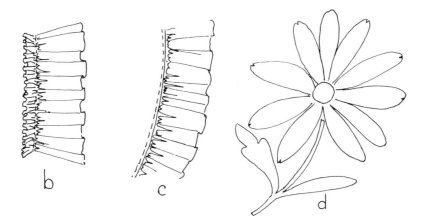

b c d

of the circle. Gather it along one edge (b). Turn ½ inch of the circle edge under. Pin and sew ruffle around the circle (c). Make and attach waistband as before, and decorate with cut-out flowers made of papers you like (d).

For still another apron, cut a waistband of crepe paper in the same way as for previous apron. Cut a piece of crepe paper as in pattern (a). Now cut a long ribbon of crepe paper, and gather the whole length, gathering enough to go all around the apron. For the apron in the illustration, use a strip 2 inches wide, and the length of an entire package of crepe paper. To put it another way, 2 inches may be cut off the end of a package (b). The resulting strip will depend on the size of the apron. Cut a double strip of crepe paper

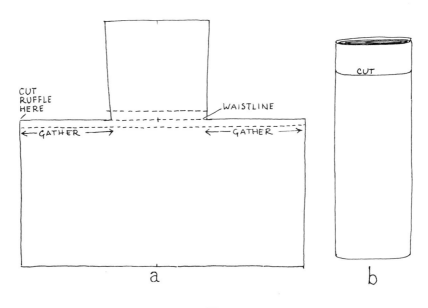

a b

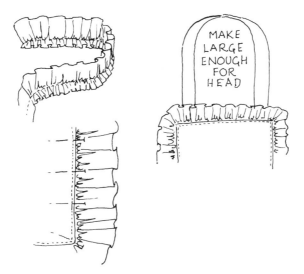

for the neckband, being careful not to cut it too long. It should leave an opening large enough for the head to go through. Gather skirt at places indicated (a). Sew ruffle around edges of skirt and top. If more flair is desired in the ruffles, stretch the edge.

Sew waistband on top of waistline (dotted line in pattern). Attach neckband to two top corners either tacking by hand or using glue. Apply decorations according to your taste. Use a second color for the ruffle.

For yet another apron, cut two pieces of crepe paper as in pattern (a), turn all edges under and top-stitch all around. Be sure to make hole for head large enough. Make a bound buttonhole as in illustration. Use a narrow strip of paper for this (b). Cut a cardboard button, and sew it on, leaving the button loose enough to get through the hole easily (c).

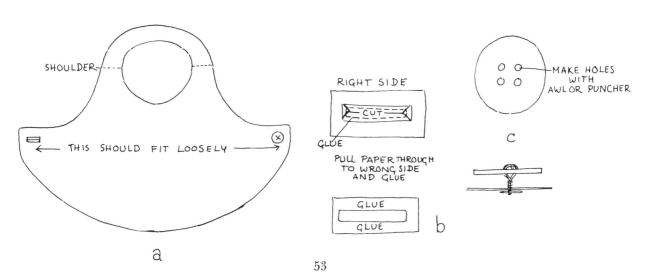

53

HATS

Though in some remote epoch hats may have been worn to shield from burning sun or pouring rain, during most of recorded history they have been worn to attract the other sex, to distract from unattractive features, to add to meagre height or subtract from excessive height—and most of all just for fun.

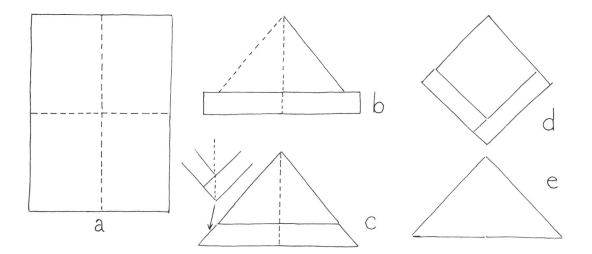

An admiral's hat is an admirable thing, and you can make one by taking a piece of paper (colored on both sides) with the proportions of three by four. Fold in half as in the illustration. Fold in half again, and open folds (a). Fold upper corners down to center fold line (b). Fold bottom margins up, one to each side (c). Overlap the ends, then fold them down (d). Fold the same ends up to meet at point (e). Add a paper plume (See Chapter 6 on birds). The head measurement should equal the long side of the paper, so if the head measurement is 24 inches then the long side of the paper should be 24 inches and the other side 18 inches.

For another hat, cut two 2/3 of a circle, as you do for cones, out of crepe paper, and sew or glue the edges together (a). Sew or glue the outer-rim edges together (b). Hold middle finger and thumb of one hand together, and pull hat through the opening by its point. If you want tighter pleats, squeeze the hat. For a ruffle around the bottom, stretch the outer rim gently.

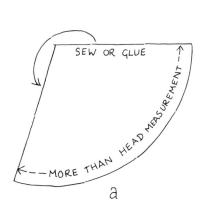

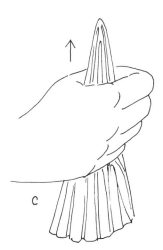

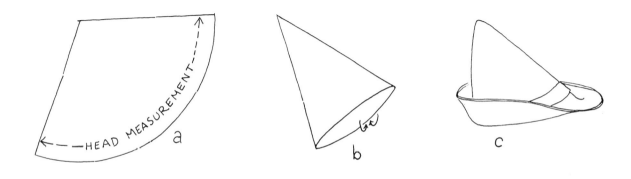

Such exciting hats exist in many variations. To make one, cut two 2/3 of a circle out of crepe paper. Check the measurement of the head because this should correspond with the dotted line measurement in the illustration (a). Glue or sew edges together (b). Glue or sew outer edges and make a hatband of crepe paper with same measurements as your head. Turn up edge of hat in back (c).

For a top hat, cut a circle of thin black poster board as shown in pattern (a). Cut tabs and bend them up on dotted line; dotted line is equal to head measurement. Make a cylinder as high as you want of the same black poster board (b). The cylinder should fit over the tabs on the rim. Make a circle of the same diameter as the cylinder. Cut tabs around the top edge of the cylinder (about ½-inch from the edge) and glue the top circle to tabs. Glue rim tabs to cylinder inside. Make a hatband of interesting paper (c).

For a Pilgrim's Hat, follow the instructions for making the top hat described in the previous paragraph, varying the shape by narrowing the crown from the brim to the top.

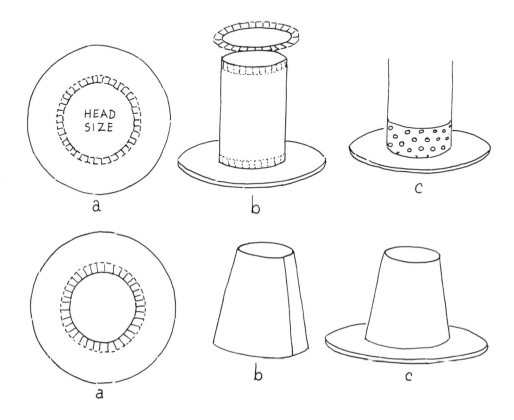

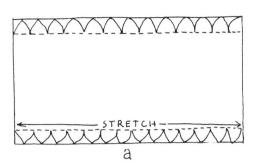

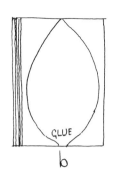

a   b   c

For another interesting hat, cut a strip of crepe paper long enough for the head size. The width should be about 10 inches (a). Cut leaf shapes along both edges; then gather on the dotted line. Stretch outer edge to frill it. Multiple-cut about fifty leaves and glue them to the hat (b). A blossom hat may be made in the same way, cutting out petals instead of leaves.

What was once called a dust bonnet, and now serves many uses, may be made by cutting large circles of crepe paper as in pattern (a). Draw as in illustration the two dotted circles on paper of one circle. Now machine stitch the two circles together along the dotted lines. Make a small cut between the dotted lines, and run a piece of elastic to fit head (¼ inch wide) between the layers. Tie or sew the ends of the elastic. Fold over and sew or glue the outer edges together. A pretty effect can be had by using two colors for the circles, and then adding a few flowers or leaves and ribbon around the gathered part (b).

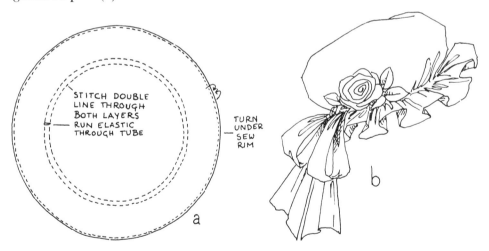

a   b

To make still another hat, the Pilgrim's Bonnet, cut two oblongs of crepe paper, one black and one white. The longest sides of the oblongs should measure about the same as the distance just below one earlobe and across the head to just below the other earlobe. The width should be the same as

57

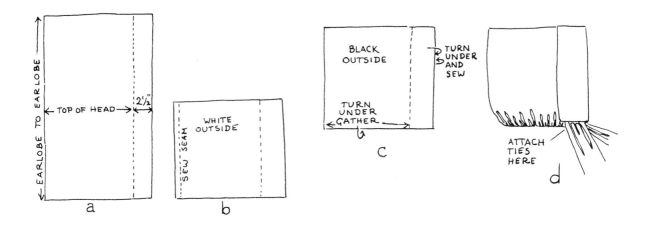

the top of the head plus 2½ inches (a). Fold the pieces in half (white outside) and sew the back seam (b). Turn black side out, and turn lower edge under ½ inch. Gather stitch on dotted line (c). Fold under front edges, and sew. Turn white "cuff" up and back. Cut two double pieces of white crepe paper long enough to tie under the chin, and attach to both corners (d).

SUN HATS

Paper makes wonderful Sun hats. Begin by cutting a large circle of thin poster board, or other pliable board. Cut two slots as in pattern (a) for ribbon. These should be about 7 inches apart, the circle being about 24 inches across. Lace a ribbon made of crepe paper (doubled and stitched along both edges through slots). The ribbon should be long enough to run around the head (and hat) and to tie under the chin. Make several roses, leaves, and a bow and attach them to the top of the hat (b). The same hat can be made much smaller to be used with a bergerette costume.

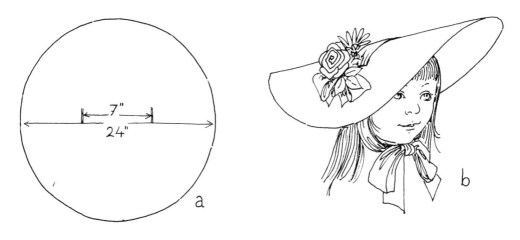

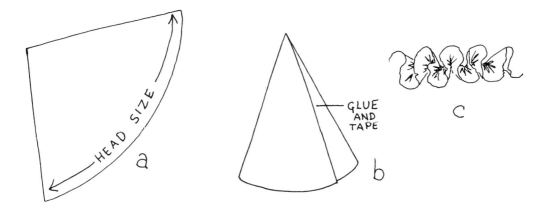

For a clown or witch hat, make a cone of thin poster board or other pliable board (a). The lower edge must measure the same as the head size. Glue and tape the edges (b). Add an edging for the clown hat; make a fringe or a ruffle, and attach it to the lower edge with glue or staples (c).

A KING'S CROWN

Where once upon a time crowns were worth a fortune and given by kings to special loved ones, now they are worn chiefly, aside from a few royal heads, by people at masquerades and other such parties, and are made of so-called junk jewelry or pinchbeck. Such crowns can be made of paper, too.

To make such a crown, use thin cardboard covered with aluminum foil, having measured the diameter of the head for which it is intended and add a ½-inch overlap on both ends. With whatever frills you plan, draw your design on the cardboard, and cut it out with a sharp knife (a). Cover with aluminum foil before fastening ends.

To cover with foil, place the cut-out crown on the back side of the foil paper so as to trace it with a pencil. Then cut it out, keeping a narrow margin. Snip margin all around configurations (b). Trace a second crown on back side of paper, cutting it now on tracing line. Glue first foil cutout to

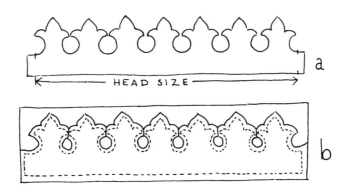

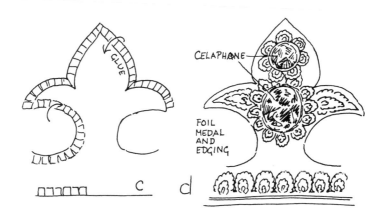

front of crown. Glue snipped margin around edges, and then glue on second foil piece as a facing (c). Attach ends with staples, or staples and glue. Decorate crown with medallions or strips of embossed gold foil—or both. Make jewels of bits of crumpled cellophane glued to gold medallions (d).

BELTS

No form of human apparel has been viewed as wholly utilitarian, not hats, surely, and certainly not belts. Belts have been girded with precious

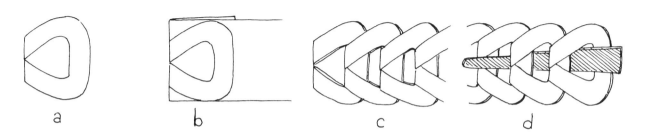

a   b   c   d

metal and studded and jeweled throughout modern history, and they may be made now simply of beautiful papers.

First draw and cut a pattern piece of cardboard as shown in the illustration (a). Trace the pattern onto thick, tough, but pliable paper, such as vellum or velour paper folded double. Draw as many links as you need to reach around the waist, plus three (each is ½ inch) (b). Cut out all the links. Make the belt by looping each link around another as in illustration (c). To fasten, overlap first and last three links, and skewer them with a pin made of thick cardboard covered with paper (d).

For another handsome belt, cut and fold enough pieces of tissue paper (yes!) to fit the waist for which it is intended. Each double link is about ¾ inch, and each piece is about 4½ inches by 4 inches (a). Fold each piece of paper in half lengthwise, then fold again, and one more time—three folds in all (b). Fold strip in half, and then fold ends to center and close (c). Link pieces together by putting the folded ends of one piece through folded ends of next piece (d). Do the same with the following piece from the opposite direction. When the belt is long enough to make four extra links, make a clasp (e). Fold a piece of the same paper as for belt links. Glue a double piece of florist's wire in the last fold of paper (f). Fold and bend and clasp around first and last four links.

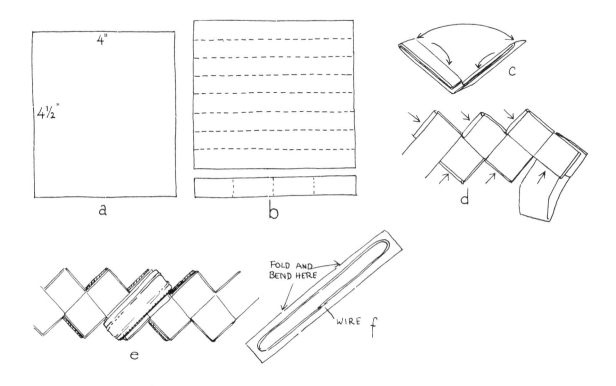

COSTUMES

Though most costumes are better made of fabric, paper and its derivatives occupy an increasingly important place. Still, one must recommend the use of cloth except for accessories. Only a few costumes are suitably made of paper, and then usually if they are made in small sizes.

A ballet dress may be made with a sleeveless leotard. Cut and gather a strip of crepe paper about one inch wide, making it long enough to go around the neck and arm holes. Sew the ruffle on. Make a few roses and other flowers and leaves of paper, and glue them around the ruffle (a).

Now cut a strip about 12 inches wide and 5 yards long, and gather it tightly. Put the leotard on the figure, and wrap the gathered strip around and around until used up. Pin the ruffle in many places to hold size (b). Remove the leotard carefully. If ruffle comes above the end of the zipper, snip through the layers of the ruffle to the end of the zipper (c).

Baste ruffle to leotard, and sew with large stitches. Make more flowers for waistline decoration. Use some long ribbons that reach to the end of the ruffle. As a variation from flowers, design a large medallion with flowing ribbons (d).

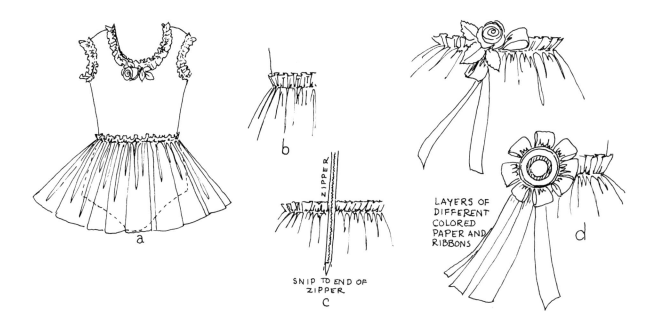

For little girls' costumes for parties and perhaps for older girls' costumes, too, there are fairy costumes made like the ballet dress but with the skirt longer and less full. Make small wings of vellum or bristol board (optional) and attach to leotard at about the point of the shoulder blades (a). Make

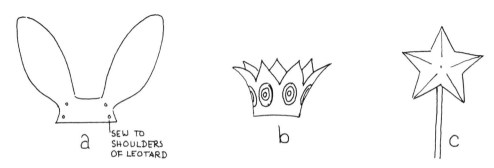

a SEW TO SHOULDERS OF LEOTARD

b

c

coronet (see section on crowns) of foil paper. Make loops for bobby pins. Make a wand of a dowel (10 inches or 12 inches) pointed up by a gold or silver star (See stars on page 157).

THE ELVES' COSTUMES

At parties elves are always welcome, and the appropriate costume to wear if you wish to be an elf is a green or brown leotard covered with leaves. Tack each leaf on with glue. Cut a 2-inch fringe of crepe paper cut in leaf shapes (a) and gather and sew it to neck and armholes. Cover rest of outfit with leaves (b). Make a cap on the model of the hat on page 56.

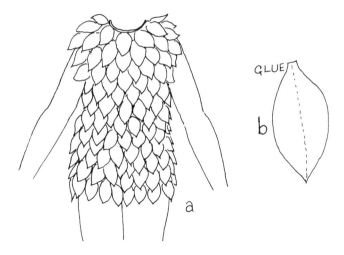

GLUE

a

b

The costume of a flower fairy can be made in much the same way as the elves' costumes, using petals instead of leaves. The headdresses are the most important part. Cut a large daisy out of bristol board (having first drawn the design on the board) and cut a hole in the middle large enough to fit around the face (a). Cut a fringe of yellow tissue paper. Tack yellow fringe to inside

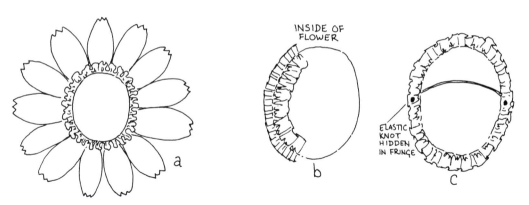

INSIDE OF FLOWER

ELASTIC KNOT HIDDEN IN FRINGE

a

b

c

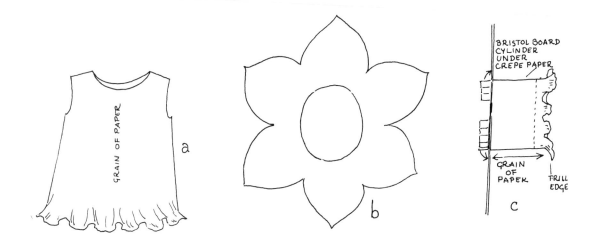

of face-hole with glue or staples. Bring fringe to outside (b). Attach an elastic to daisy, large enough to go around the head (c). By using yellow board and a brown center, the result will be a black-eyed susan.

Another delightful flower is the daffodil, and the flower supplies the theme for a costume. Start by making a simple crepe paper dress (a). Frill the edges by stretching them. Cut a six-petalled yellow board as for daisy (b). Make the trumpet part of a piece of yellow crepe paper over bristol board. Make a cylinder to fit face hole. Glue seam. Attach tabs to inside of the face hole. Frill the edge.

PILGRIMS' COSTUMES

Paper is used for making the Pilgrims' hat, bonnet, collars, and cuffs. In making the man's collar, use thin bristol board or vellum cut according to pattern (a). For the lady's collar, cut of the same board according to pattern. Pin or tie together at throat (b). Cut the cuffs as shown in pattern. Staple or glue the edges (c).

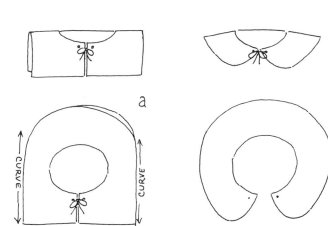

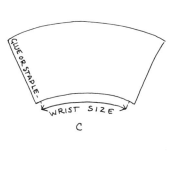

MASKS FOR FUN

Ideally, mystery confronts you when you are approached by someone wearing a mask—and in its happiest form when this happens at a masquerade party. The simplest masks to make are the flat ones made out of bristol board or poster board. Here the artist has free rein to use any design he can dream up.

Use cut-out effects, and give yourself full freedom in cutting and bending the nose and mouth (a). Glue on pieces for interesting features. Attach an elastic headband. Where you cut holes, reinforce with Mystik tape (b).

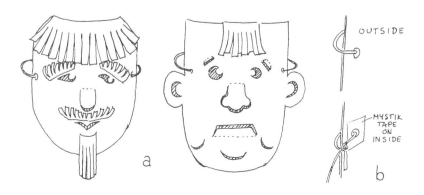

Even simpler masks are those made from brown paper bags from the grocery store. Just cut out a face and decorate with any grotesqueries you like. Why not add a pluck of fringe for hair!

PAPIER-MACHE

Excellent masks may be made of papier-mâché (see page 65). Here we deal with a much more complicated process. There are several ways to use papier-mâché. Here we describe the two easiest ways for making masks. One way is to use plasticene or modelling clay to create the model of the mask (a). Rub it carefully with a thin layer of vaseline. Then stick first layer of paper to vaseline-coated surface. Now build up several layers of glue and paper, criss-crossing the paper in all directions and being careful to make an even layer all over (b). Let everything dry thoroughly before removing the mask. In lifting the mask off the model, pry all around the edges with a knife, lifting slowly and carefully.

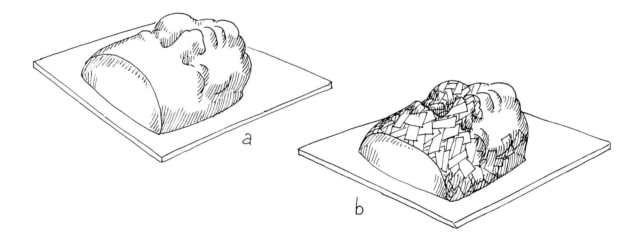

A mask for the entire head can be made in somewhat the same way, though it must be cut in two (front and back) along the sides to be removable (c) and then taped together again. Trim the edges.

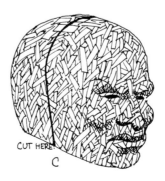

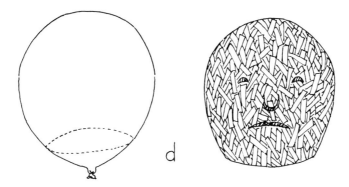

d

Another whole-head mask can be made using a balloon. Choose a balloon with this in mind and blow it to the size you want. Use a felt-tip pen or other marker to indicate where the opening will be after the mask is finished (d). Cover with glue and paper directly on the balloon (no vaseline) above the mark. After the mask has dried completely, remove the balloon. Cut in the features. If opening for head should be too small, strip the back edge until mask fits over the head. Trim the edges.

A simple way to make papier-mâché is to use gummed paper tape. Cut hundreds of little strips of tape, and use a wet sponge to apply them to a model that has been rubbed with vaseline, then covered with a lining paper. Dampen this paper and each strip of paper, dampen the layer of tape, and then all the next layers of tape until structure seems strong enough. Let dry thoroughly before removing from model.

Papier-mâché masks are only moderately interesting until they are decorated. Before decorating, however, they must be thoroughly dry. Once dry, you may apply lacquers or oil paints, and glue on paper hair or a beard or adorn them in other ways.

CHAPTER 5

BOXES, BASKETS
AND GIFT WRAPPING

Time out of mind, the box has been most especially prized by woman because it is essentially a household object and thus under her dominion. Since aside from sewing sails, needlework has been mostly women's work, they have had need for an orderly way of stowing the needles and threads and thimbles and swatches and patches and other important ingredients of stitchery. What evolved may as well be called a box.

Women, being as they are, took no time at all in deciding to make the box beautiful, and of course presently were vying with each other to see whose would be most elegantly decorative. They covered their boxes with silk, embroidered them, and encrusted them with jewels precious and semi-precious. All the differences had to do with status considerations.

The snuff box is perhaps the most elegant box of all as we see from examples surviving from the 17th and 18th centuries. During these centuries, no gentleman could possibly have appeared socially without a small box of snuff upon which had been lavished all sorts of jewels. Though the practice of sniffing the powder of tobacco for stimulation was widespread during these centuries, the value of the snuff box rested equally on its opportunity to display *bijouterie* and was surrounded by extremely obvious pretensions.

Traditionally, the jewel box has been the most glamorous because of the presumed value of its contents. Of course such treasures must be placed in a receptacle of suitable elegance. That the jewel box was not taken lightly we see from the ones that were made for Marie Antoinette—one at Versailles, another at Windsor Castle, and both the work of three artists: Schwerdfeger, a fine cabinet-marker; Degault, an excellent miniature painter; and Thomire, a skilled chaser.

Elegance characterized many of the knife boxes, especially though not exclusively those designed by Hepplewhite, Adam, and Sheraton. These were for the storage of silver spoons, forks and knives. They appeared in many forms from flat-topped boxes and vase shapes to those with a lid on a sloped front for the display and easy availability of silver stored on stepped shelves extending upwards from front to back. They were of artistic design and their beauty was partly due to the color and sheen of the mahogany and satinwood used with embellishments such as marqueterie and boxwood edging.

Boxes can be serious or frivolous and gay. In long ago days there was the patch box in which milady secreted tiny appliqués for her face, and in modern days there is the powder box, or compact.

A wonderful box, perhaps the most wonderful, is the mailbox. Perhaps this box is special because you know that one letter you find there may change your life—make you rich or poor, famous or infamous, honored or dishonored, loved or unloved, blessed with an offspring or deprived of a beloved.

Wondering about your future, you may find the answer in a box.

If a box sounds humble, so does its cousin, the basket. This is a modification of the design, usually with handles for carrying. As it is humble, so are its uses: container for school lunches, school books, sewing and knitting supplies; a pocketbook; a carrier for swim suit and towel; and while traveling a container for reading and writing material.

Boxes, early and late, have served practical purposes. After rising to great heights because of the precious metals and the incrustation of priceless jewels, they have risen again with the development of remarkable papers that sometimes can be thought of in the same class as famous tapestries. The new papers range from extraordinarily colored ones and ones with three-dimensional effects to those which suggest metal surfaces or remarkable fabrics. And with developments such as these, boxes become treasure chests again, pretty or flamboyant, worthy of the treasures they are designed to contain, and worthy even if they contain only mystery.

Gift wrappings partake of the same artistic qualities and implied mystery. Surely a beautiful wrapping gives pleasure by promising a thing of beauty inside. Would someone with the good taste to choose such a wrapping select anything less than a beautiful gift? If necessity forced him to choose an extravagant wrapping and a modest gift, this would still demonstrate his wish that both might be in keeping.

In making boxes it is best to begin with a square one. Draw a pattern on thin cardboard as in the illustration, all squares identical, in this example with 3-inch sides. With a sharp knife cut along the solid lines. Then score on dotted lines (a). Fold up side pieces on scored lines (b). Bend and secure corners together with strips of glued tape or strong paper using Elmer's glue (c).

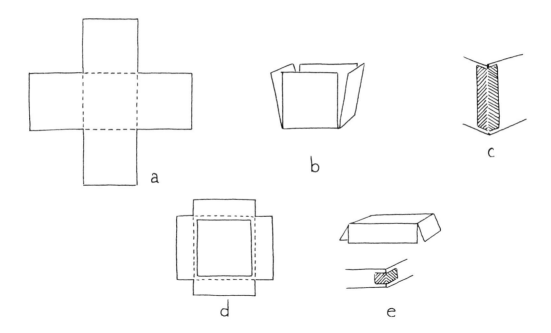

For the top, draw a pattern on the same kind of cardboard. Score dotted lines, and cut others (d). Draw dotted line according to dimensions, plus 1/16 of an inch (in this case 3 inches plus 1/16 inch on each side). Draw the side pieces ¾ inch to 1 inch wide. Finish in the same way as the box (e).

For another very useful square box, draw a pattern on bristol board (the sides of the squares being 4 inches), cut out on the solid lines of the illustration. Score on dotted lines (a). Bend sides up on scored lines, then bend tabs on sides toward inside of box (b). Glue tabs to inside of edge of sides (c).

For the top, draw the pattern on bristol board. Score dotted lines and cut the others. Draw dotted line 1/16 inch outside of size of box, which makes the box 4-1/16 inches on each side (d). Draw the side pieces ¾ inch to 1 inch wide. Finish in the same way as the box (e).

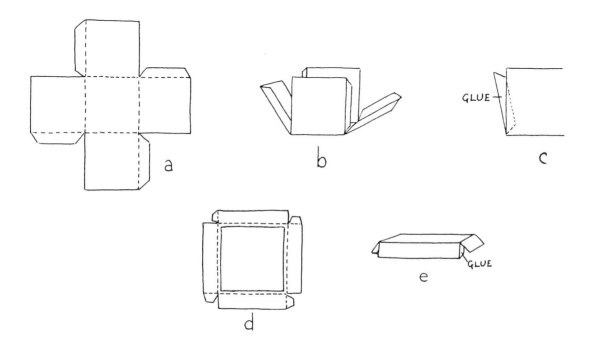

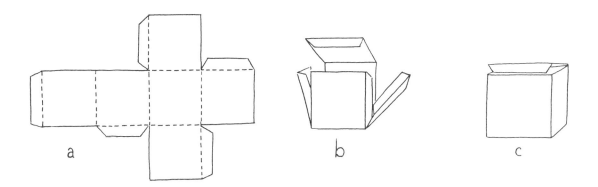

a   b   c

For still a third square box, draw pattern on bristol board with all squares equal, the sides being 2 inches. Cut out along the solid lines. Then score dotted lines (a). Fold the four side pieces up on scored lines. Bend tabs on sides inward, and glue to inside of edge of side pieces (b). Then fold top over to cover box. Turn tab inward, and tuck in to close (c).

OBLONG BOXES

Draw pattern on thin cardboard. The sides and bottom should be equal. The sides of the ends should equal the width of the bottom of the box, in this case 3 inches (a). Cut out on solid lines. Score on dotted lines. Bend all sides up on scored lines, and secure corners with strips of glue tape or strong paper affixed with glue (b). For the top, draw a pattern on the thin cardboard. The scoring line should be 1/16 inch outside the size of the box. Draw side pieces ¾ inch to 1 inch wide. Finish the same way as the box (c).

For second and third oblong boxes, make in same way as the second and third square boxes, using measurements of desired length, width, and height.

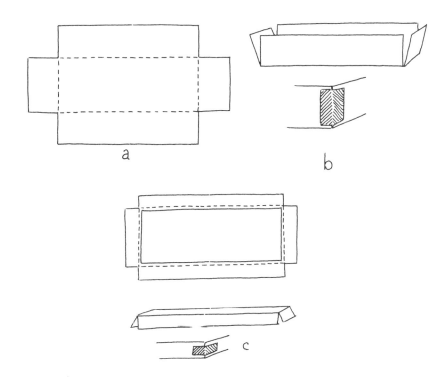

a   b

c

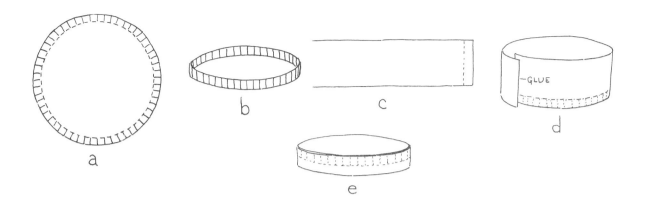

ROUND BOXES

Using a compass draw a circle for bottom of box. Draw second circle ½ inch wider around first circle. Cut out on dotted line. Score on solid line (a). Cut notches from dotted line to solid line. Bend resulting tabs upward (b). Now cut straight piece of board long enough to reach around circle, plus overlap of ½ inch. The width of the strip is the height of the box (c). Glue tabs to the inside of the strip. Glue end overlap (d). For top do the same things as for bottom of box, but measure circle ⅛ inch wider, and make strip only ¾ inch wide (e).

To make a second round box, draw circle for the bottom, and cut out (a). Cut a side strip long enough to go around the circle with ½ inch overlap (b). Glue overlap. Attach strip of glue-paper tape around strip, leaving half of tape over edge (c). Snip notches all around, and stick down on bottom of circle (d). For the top, do the same as for bottom. Make top circle 1/16 inch wider, and make strip only ¾ inch wide.

Round boxes may be made out of paper tubes, in which case two tops are required, to be made like the top for the first round box described, using a diameter of 1/16 inch greater than the diameter of the tube.

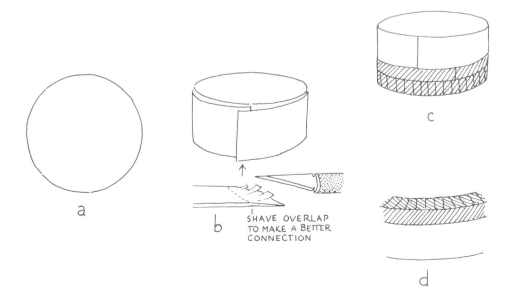

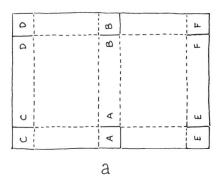

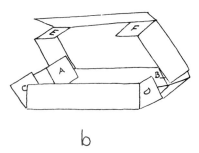

a

b

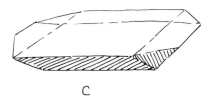

c

ODD-SHAPED BOXES

These can be made in the same basic way as the round boxes. Accurate measuring with tape measure or the outlines of the shapes is important.

For a folded box, a soft one suitable for candies, cookies, and gifts, draw pattern on inside of bristol board, first having glued decorative paper to outside of board and spreading the glue thinly and evenly (a). For the pattern, the lines around the rectangle and down the center of the rectangle are equal. The solid lines should be cut, the dotted lines scored. Glue A to A, B to B, and so forth (b). Fold box up for storage on dotted lines (c).

For a second such folded box in triangular form use bristol and make according to illustrations (a). Decorate with fancy paper, paint, or stickers. This is very good for the packaging of candies, cookies, and for hanging small gifts on the Christmas tree (b).

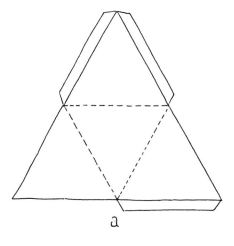

a

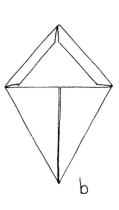

b

DECORATIVE PAPER (HOW TO COVER BOXES WITH)

By now you will have noticed that many beautiful things may be made from otherwise mundane materials. Here boxes previously used for shoes, stationery, oatmeal, cornmeal, salt, and much else, turn out to have a Cinderella-like glamor. Paper rolls from foil or plastic wrap, rolls from paper towels or toilet paper (the last are all, plus or minus 1½ inches in diameter) become primary materials in paper artistry. Mailing tubes are larger and have their special uses.

When using such materials it is important to strip off all stickers and labels, being careful not to tear supporting pieces of paper or tape on corners. Use tip of knife to lift up sticker ends. When only glued-down paper remains, boxes are ready for new paper and decorations. Make use of whatever gift-wrap paper interests you, or of gold foil strips, medallions, paper lace, doilies, fancy stickers or cut-outs. A subtle and effective touch can be achieved by giving the wrapping a resemblance to the gift inside.

The right amount of paper can be measured by putting the box on its side on paper ½ inch away from the edge. Make small mark at corners. Then roll box one way and another to mark (a). Put glue on bottom of box, and place it on the wrong side of the paper (b). With scissors cut out corner pieces leaving tabs on both sides of two corresponding side pieces. Glue paper to these two sides of box. Glue ½ inch margins to inside of box and tabs to last two sides. Glue paper to these sides, and the ½-inch margins to inside of box. Trim off any surplus paper. Follow the same procedure to cover the box top.

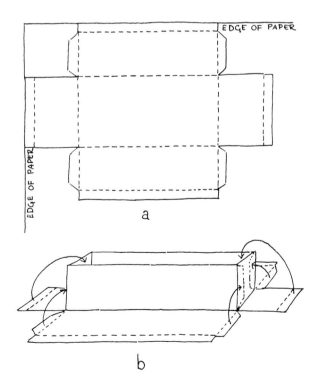

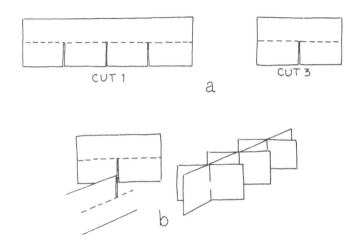

To make compartments for a square or oblong box, measure the box's length and width. Decide how many compartments you want, and cut your pieces of cardboard accordingly. If you want eight compartments in a shoe box, for example, cut one piece as long as the box, and three pieces as wide. The pieces should also match the depth of the box (a). Cut slots in the pieces as in pattern (b). Cover each piece with bright glossy paper, and recut slots. Line box with the same glossy paper. Fit all the compartment pieces together, and put into box. For added color, line each compartment with tissue paper in colors complementary to the outside paper.

To line a square or oblong box, cut a piece of paper of the same dimensions as the box. Cut two tabs on two corresponding sides. Glue them to inside of two other sides. Trim off excess paper. Put glue all around the inside edge of box (c).

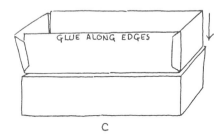

Cover a nest of boxes (square ones most appropriate). Find or make boxes of two, three, four, five, or six inches square, or oblongs that fit into each other. Cover each box with a different but related design; for example, use five different floral papers.

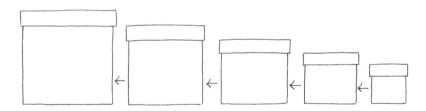

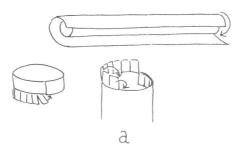

a

For the tube boxes, first cover the tops in the same way as the covering of a round box top. Cover the tube. Roll a piece of paper around the tube, leaving a margin at each end. Cut tabs, and glue them to the inside of the tube (a). Glue one top to one end of tube. Use the other as a cover (b). Decorate with embossed gold strip or floral stickers.

For a round box, cut a circle of paper for bottom. Leave a ½-inch margin in which to cut tabs (a). Cut a strip as wide as the depth of the box, leaving a ½-inch margin. The strip should be as long as the circumference of the box with overlap added (b). Glue circle to bottom of box. Fold tabs up, and glue them to the side of box (c). Glue one end of side strip to side (d). Put a line of glue all around the bottom edge (on tabs). Fold tabs to inside of box, and glue (e). Follow the same steps in covering the top. Decorate the box with items such as doilies and embossed stickers. Line the box by gluing a circle of paper in the bottom. Glue a strip around the side. Trim off top edge (f).

Cover odd-shaped boxes by following these instructions, always keeping in mind the extra ½ inch for making tabs to be glued under the overlapping piece.

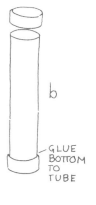

b

GLUE
BOTTOM
TO
TUBE

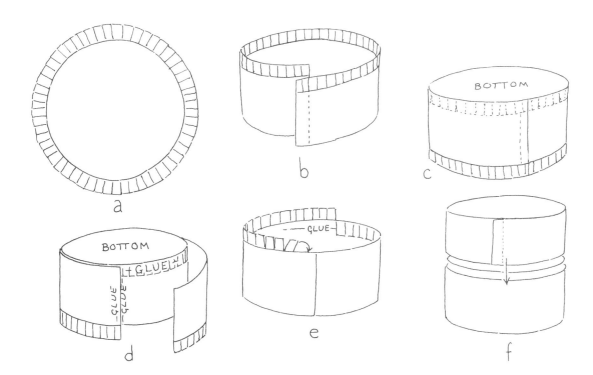

a

b

c

d

e

f

FOLDED BASKET I

Take square of origami-type paper and fold in half straight across twice (a), and diagonally twice. Bring two opposite points together (b). Then bring the other two points to the middle. Now fold top point down on dotted line. Do same on reverse (c). Take a new strip of paper (same length as side of

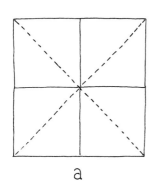

a

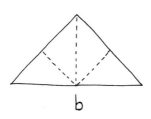

b

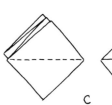

c

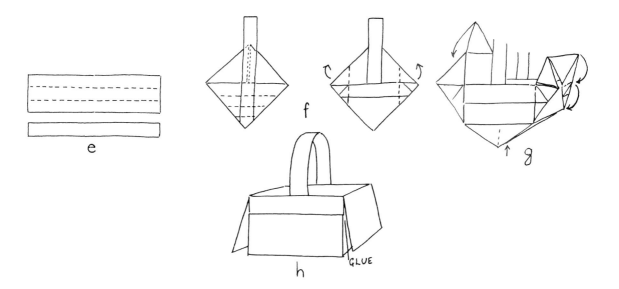

square) and fold it on dotted lines (d). Take one end of strip and fold it together with point upward on dotted lines as in illustration (e). Now fold side points backward on dotted lines (f). Pull top points outward, and fold them down and over (g). This forms the square basket. Now fold the points back to form rim, and to inside of basket. Tack corners down with dot of glue (h).

FOLDED BASKET II

Start again with a square of paper, folding it in half, and then again in half. Fold it again in opposite directions so that 16 squares result when it is unfolded. Now fold diagonally on dotted lines (a). (Shaded area is bottom of box.) Fold corners down (A). Then fold down on BC lines twice (b). Glue down sides, and attach handle to either of opposite sides using staples or glue (d).

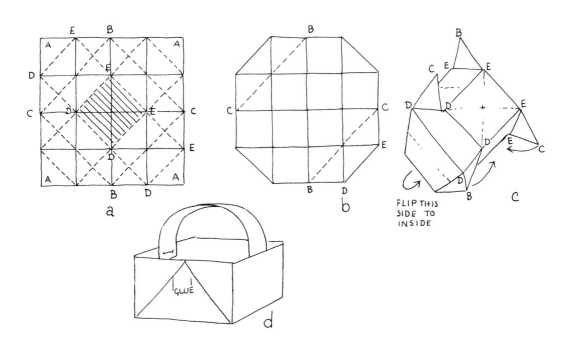

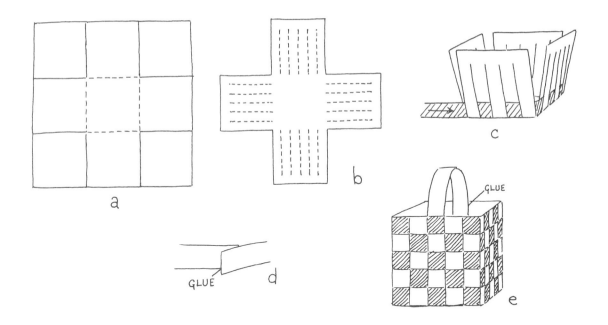

WOVEN BASKET

Take square of paper and fold as indicated on dotted lines. Cut out corners as indicated on dotted lines (a). Draw four lines evenly spaced on inside of each side piece. Then cut on lines, leaving an even margin along outer edge of each side piece (b). Cut strips of another color, the same width as margin, and cut side pieces (so that small squares will result). Fold side pieces up. Starting at the bottom, weave strips around sides (c). Tack strip ends with dots of glue (d). To make handle, take double strip of second color of paper. Weave ends down inside basket. Tack at basket edge with glue (e).

WOVEN STRING BASKET

Take a piece of thick cardboard, and cut circle of dimension according to the size of basket you wish. With an awl make evenly spaced holes plus or minus ½ inch apart all around circle (a). With paper weave string up and

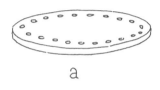

a

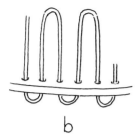

b

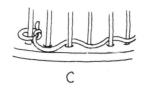

c

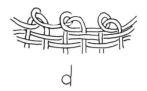

d

down through board. Pull tight on bottom of board, and leave loops to desired height (b) for finished basket. Start weaving string in and out, alternating each row (c). Tie knot around first upright. Double-weave last row by looping around upright loops (d). Paint basket with spray paint if that seems to offer more possibility for self expression.

GIFT WRAPPING

Many artistic effects can be realized with the use of commercial gift wrappings and ribbons. They are the products of skillful artists. As gift wrappings are available in a great variety, so are tissue papers to be had in a wide range of colors, and the possibility of combining the two opens the way to much originality, as does the application of paper flowers, glued to the package or intertwined with the ribbon bows.

Choosing two or three complementary colors, place the object to be wrapped in the center of the paper, and fold the pieces up around the sides. Bunch them on top, tie together, and fluff up the paper peaks.

To wrap a round gift such as a jar of jelly, roll a piece of paper around jar, leaving considerable overlap at both ends (roughly the radius of the circle). Fold pleats one over the other as illustrated (a).

To make wrapping easier and neater, it is helpful to use small pieces of sticky tape as you go. Fold ends of square cornered packages as indicated (b).

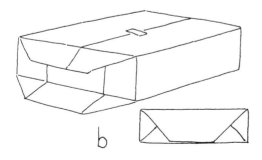

b

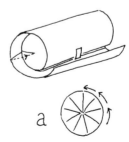

a

CHAPTER 6

FLOWERS, PLANTS AND TREES

So great is the love most people feel for flowers that from time immemorial they have shown their reluctance to let go of Fall flowers by attempting to contrive artificial blossoms, which if not as lovely and ethereal as those of the garden, have reminiscent value.

Papers of all kinds and colors are now easily found. Delicate and beautiful papers come as a decorative filler in ladies' stockings and other fashion products. If these seem strange starting points for the creation of art, it should be remembered that great sculptors usually start with clay-like products such as plaster and plasticene. What the artist does with the materials is what counts. As a noted hat designer once said when asked how she could ask $2,500 for a hat that consisted only of a piece of ribbon worth at most two dollars: "Oh, the hat is worth $2,500. The ribbon is free!"

Though flowers made of paper are the most generally admired simulations, there have been many others. The Egyptains painted them on linen, and fabricated them with shavings of painted horn; the Romans made similar imitations elegant with appliqués of gold and silver; the South Americans looked to the feathers of colorful birds; the Chinese, among other peoples of the East, attempted to keep flowers all year round by recording them on rice paper in superb renderings.

Italians are frequently found concerning themselves with the kindred subjects of flowers and fruit, whether in selling them or painting them or singing about them; this shows the impetus of the centuries, because the Italians had long been breeding flowers and after the season counterfeiting them before their artistic skills passed over the border to the French.

Little is known about earlier French interest, but in the 1700's French artists and craftsmen took the art away from the Italians, and became known worldwide as creators of artificial flowers. Later, as a result of turbulent politics, French artists crossed the Channel, bringing their art with them, and they or their descendants eventually crossed the Atlantic to America.

Artificial flowers may be bought in many stores, but perhaps the most beautiful—in any case the most interesting such flowers—are those you make yourself. As ever in the art of creating beautiful things with paper and scissors, guidelines are given, and then the artist is off on his own adventure. How about making a peony?

PEONIES OF PAPER

The ideal paper is the soft, thin, crisp paper used in packing women's stockings; sometimes it is a most delicate pink paper, though the white paper will be found suitable, as well as most kinds of tissue paper.

Start by cutting several petals in various irregular shapes, seven or eight large ones and about twenty shorter and smaller ones (a). Now cut six strips of magenta red tissue paper. Make pistils by folding the strips on both sides toward the center (b). Then pinch the point to give the pistil a two-sided effect. Squeeze the six pistils together in a bunch. Use a few drops of glue on the pistil stems to hold them together. Wrap a strip of green coated paper tightly around pistil stems, again using a few dots of glue. Twist the green paper to a point.

Now cut a strip of yellow tissue paper. Fold strip double, lengthwise. Then with scissors cut narrow fringe to about ¼ inch from edge, the cuts about ⅛ inch apart (c). Now cut the entire strip lengthwise on fold line. Wrap

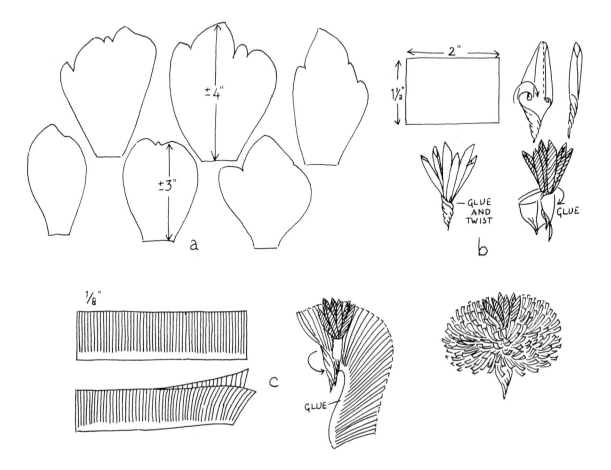

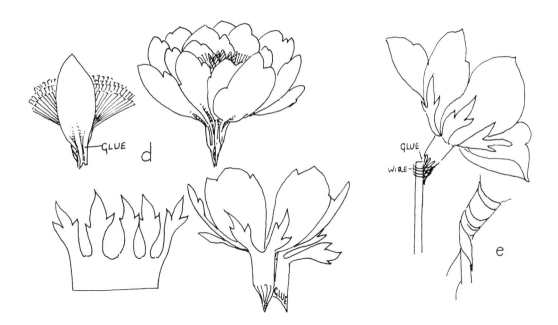

resulting fringe around pistil segment until it is used up, using a dot of glue as you go. Then fluff the stamens to give a pom-pom effect. Always pinch the lower part of each finished segment to make it as tight and sturdy as possible. Now wrap the smaller petals around the stamens, using one small drop of glue at the base of each petal (d). Repeat the process, turning the flower as you go until all the petals are used up. Use large petals last. Cut a strip of green coated paper for the calyx. Cut irregular shapes as illustrated. Wrap calyx around petal ends, using dots of glue to secure. Pinch and shape to a point.

Attach your blossom to bamboo or wire (preferably at an angle) by wrapping green crepe-paper ribbon or florists' tape tightly around calyx, then spiraling down the stem (e). Secure tape or ribbon with bit of glue at both ends of stem.

ROSES

Tissue paper is effective, too, in the making of roses. You do well to use all one color (pink, yellow, red, white) or two shades of one color. The darker shades should be used for the buds and centers, the lighter ones for the outer petals of the full rose.

To make the bud or center of the rose, take a strip of tissue paper, and fold it in half lengthwise (a). Then start at one end, rolling and gathering the bottom edge (b). Pinch stem as tight as you can. Shape a bud as you go. For solidity put a drop of glue on stem part every so often as you roll. You roll to the end of the strip, folding down upper corner of end diagonally (c). The resulting bud can be used as is, or petals can be added to form a full rose.

85

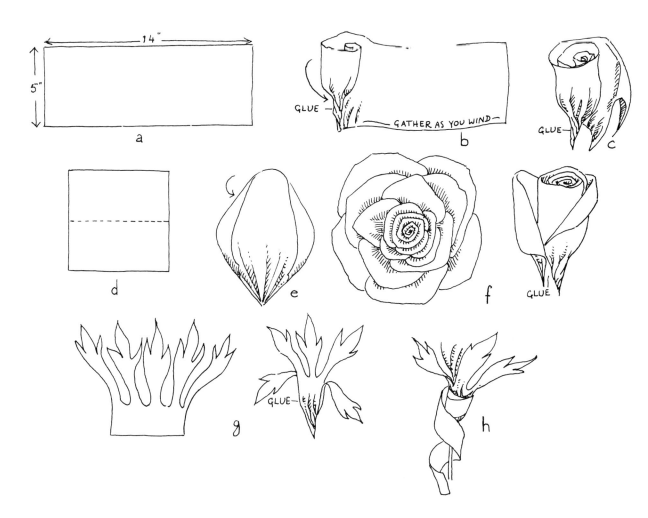

Make petals by taking squares of tissue paper and folding them in half (d). Now soft-fold sides back, gather whole lower edge, and twist it to a point (e). Make ten or twelve of these petals. Place a dot of glue at the base of each petal, assemble petals around bud, and press tightly around base of flower (f). The calyx should be cut out of green coated paper for both the bud and the flower as shown in illustration (g).

Wrap calyx strip around rose and secure with drops of glue, pinching tightly. Attach flower to stick, bamboo, or wire (h). Wrap florists' tape or green crepe paper tightly around stem and calyx. Apply a drop of glue again to secure binding. Wrap stem again of you like, adding a few rose leaves. (See Leaves, page 95.)

WILD ROSES

The petals for a wild rose should be made of sturdier paper—thin-coated paper or pink or white bond. Begin by making the center of pale green tissue.

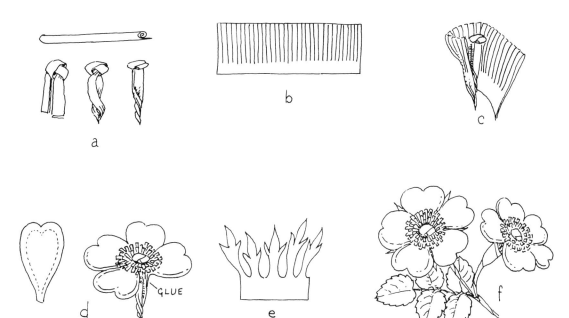

Knot a rolled-up strip of tissue paper much as you would yarn or string (a). Fold ends down and twist to a point. Flatten knot to form "button." Take strip of yellow tissue paper, folding double lengthwise. Cut very fine fringe to about ¼-inch from edge (b) and wrap around center piece. Pinch edge tightly as you go, using a little glue to secure (c).

Now come the petals. Cut half a dozen out of the pink or magenta or white-coated paper. Make them more or less heart shaped, taking care to score them lightly on the wrong side of the paper, using dotted lines for guidance (d).

Cut a calyx as for the previous roses (e) and attach blossoms to wires. (Wire is especially suitable here because of the nature of the flower.) Make several, and attach them alternately to stem (f).

STALK-LIKE FLOWERS

In nature, Hesperis (Sweet Rocket) comes in all shades of pink through lavender and almost to purple. It is suggested that you use several shades of one color of tissue paper—as many as four or five. This flower takes quite a bit of intricate work, but the results are rewarding. An imaginative and patient flower artist can make many different floral stalks, using the same basic method, introducing different colors. They may be small or large, the size is up to the artist.

You will need green buds (1), buds with the dark shade tips (2), buds with the next lighter shade tips (3), flowers in various shades (4). The greatest delicacy in color can be achieved by using two shades over each other (a).

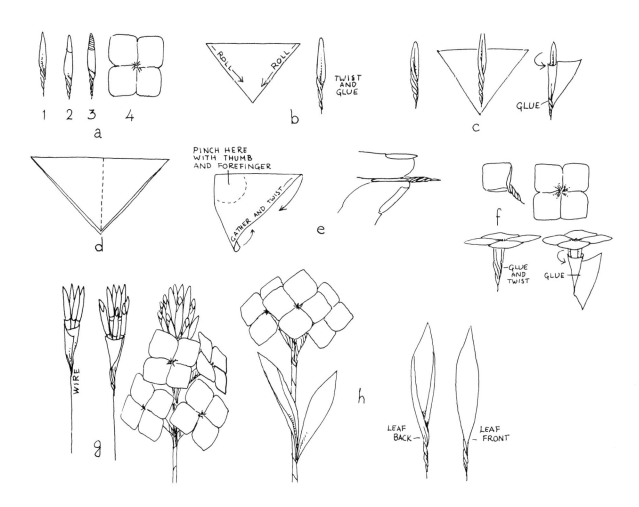

Make the first buds, perhaps six, of green tissue paper. Take small double triangles of tissue paper, folding sides inward and then rolling up tight to a point. Twist lower part for stem (b). Use dot of glue to make the stem firm. Make the next of the buds the same way but of the dark tissue paper. Finish by wrapping a single triangle of the same green tissue paper around the lower part of bud, and twisting to tight point (c). Use a dot of glue to make the stem firm. Do next four buds the same way, using tissue paper of a lighter shade.

The flowers can be made by cutting eight squares, four each of two shades of tissue paper. Put the darker colored squares on top of the lighter shades (d). Fold diagonally to form triangles. For each petal, start by folding points, of each double triangle back (e). Then hold resulting point between thumb and forefinger, and twist remaining paper to a tight point. Do this four times to make four petals for each flower.

Put flowers together by bunching the four petal stems together (use glue here) and wrap a green tissue paper triangle around them (f). Make four flowers of this combination of colors, and four of another combination this same way. Combine buds and flowers as in illustration (g), using triangles of green tissue paper, glue, and wire. Begin with the green buds at tip of wire, and then do the other buds. Attach leaves below the flowers. Leaves are made by folding triangles of green tissue paper much the same way as with the buds, but pressed flat (h).

COMPOSITE FLOWERS

Daisies, black-eyed Susans, sunflowers, and single chrysanthemums can be made in the same way. Use crisp paper, white bond or coated paper for daisies—and yellow-coated or glossy for black-eyed Susans. Tissue paper serves for centers or "eyes." Use wire for stem.

On the wrong side of the paper, lightly draw and score petals (a). Cut out petals. Make eye by taking a piece of tissue paper (yellow for daisies, dark brown for black-eyed Susans). Fold it in half lengthwise, and cut a fine fringe (b) all the way across strip, leaving a ¼-inch margin. Attach one end of fringe to wire with glue, and then wrap whole strip around center. Shape as you go, and use dots of glue to hold it firm. Now attach petal strip around center, using glue. Try not to have petals overlap completely (c). Cut a calyx of green crepe paper (d). Wrap calyx strip around flower base tightly, using a bit of glue. Finish with short piece of green crepe paper "ribbon" and glue.

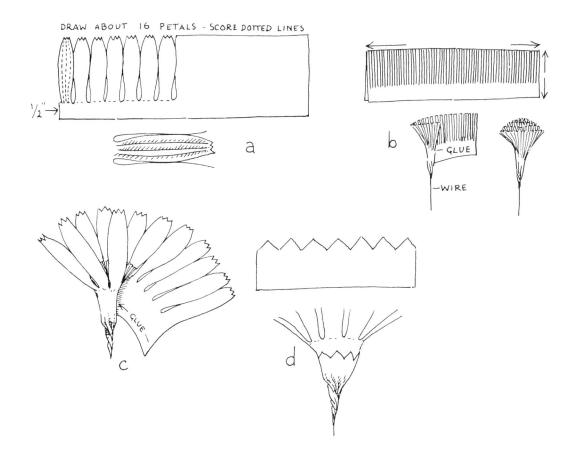

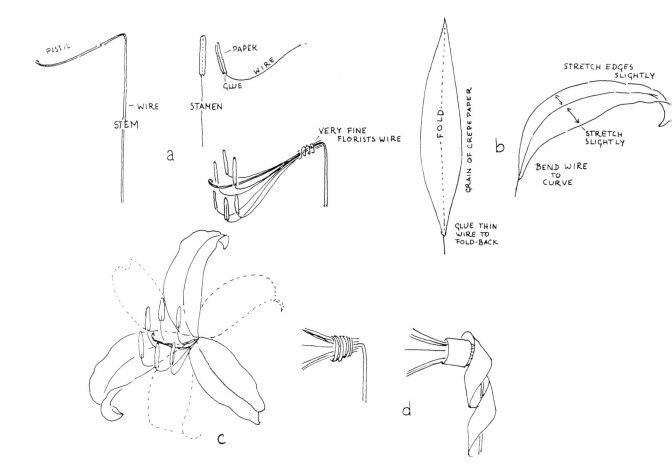

LILIES AND TULIPS

Most bulb flowers are basically the same and are easy to make. Daffodils have their trumpets, but these are not difficult to make. Crepe paper is ideal for such flowers because of its stretchable quality.

The lily's stalk will be made of the thickest florists' wire. This wire has the advantage that it can be bent so that the flower will be at the proper angle, and it can also serve for the pistil (a). Start by making six stamens of fine cotton-covered wire (white) and make anthers of small rolled pieces of dark red or maroon tissue paper and slip them on ends of wires. Attach with bit of glue, and bend back wire. Attach six stamens to pistil with very fine florists' wire. Make six petals, cutting them from white crepe paper. Follow illustration, cutting on crosswise stretch of paper. Fold through center (b) carefully stretching paper at points marked X to give petals shape. Attach three petals as indicated in illustration, and add the other three as indicated by illustration's dotted line (c). Use marker to make small dots on throat of flower (cherry red). Attach green crepe paper ribbon and finish flower-stem connection (d).

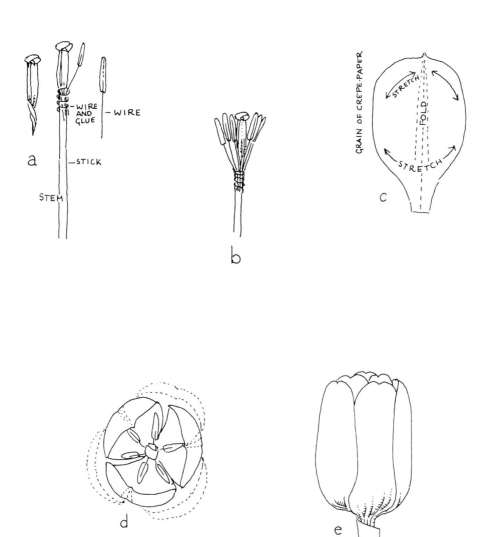

To make tulips, follow generally the instructions for the lilies. However, here a dowel may be used for a stem (a 3/16-inch dowel). Make the pistil by putting a knot in the middle of a strip of pale green tissue, and flattening knot as for the wild rose. Twist end to a point (a). Make anthers black, and use short pieces of wire. Do not bend anthers back. Attach stamens to pistil and dowel stem as for lily (b). Use glue for extra strength. Make petals as for lily, but follow illustration for shape, and stretch points (c). Attach petals to stem with wire (d). Tulips can be almost any color except blue or green. Cover both petal ends and dowel with light green crepe paper "ribbon," using bits of glue to secure (e).

91

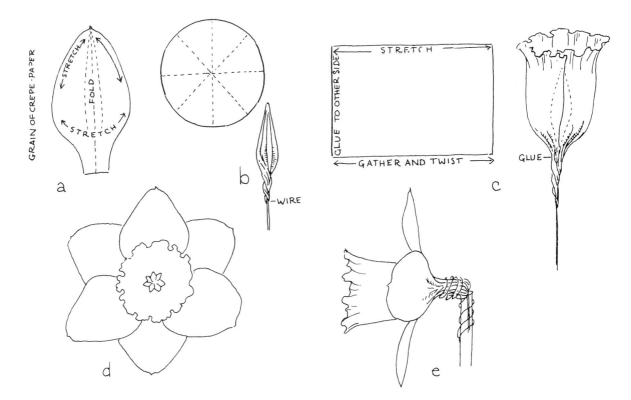

DAFFODILS

Make six petals of yellow crepe paper as for lily. Follow illustration for shape and stretch points (a). Make pistil by cutting small circle of palest yellow tissue paper. Fold on dotted lines, and twist to a point (b). Attach to a wire. Make trumpet of yellow crepe paper (c). Use glue sparingly to close cylinder. Next frill trumpet around upper edge, and gather and twist lower edge around pistil and wire. Use dot of glue to secure. Now add petals as for lilies. Fan the petals straight out (d). Wrap green crepe paper ribbon around junction of flower and stem (e) and then down stem. Always use dot of glue to secure ends.

FANTASY FLOWERS

Flowers that derive from fantasy rather than nature may be most easily made of crepe paper or tissue paper, but the fantasy may be heightened by using printed paper, gift wrap, or even newspaper. Foil can be used for a glamorous effect. Since this represents a departure from nature, any and all colors may be used to achieve fantastic effects. There are endless ways of making fantasy flowers, of course (over-sized roses and daisies achieve a stunning effect), but the guidelines for making a few will get the artist started.

To make pom-poms make many (at least ten) circles of tissue paper in graduating sizes (a). Use one or many colors as you wish. Snip edges all

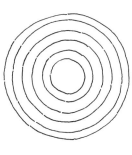

a

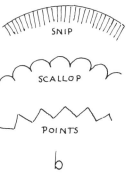

SNIP

SCALLOP

POINTS

b

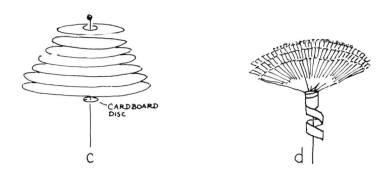

around, or scallop or cut points (b). Thread a wire with eye at one end through center of all the circles (c). Pull them up to eye, and bind tightly around eye with crepe paper "ribbon." Secure with glue (d).

For the fringe type make fringe of tissue or crepe paper (a). Turn inside out for loops, or use only clipped or cut or curled crepe paper (b). Wrap one end around wire with eye as for daffodils. Secure with glue, and wind rest of strip around center, securing with glue as you go (c).

The petal type is made much the same way as the fringe type, however, do not make the strip so long that a less full effect is achieved (a). Arrange petal strip around wire with eye (b), finish off with ribbon or tape (c). And for the combination type (d) make a center like that for the pom-poms, and then add an outer strip like that for petal type, finishing in the same way.

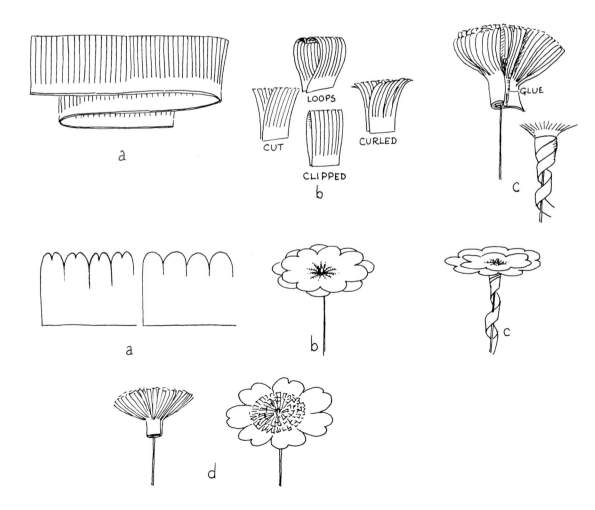

PLANTS AND THEIR LEAVES

Plants, as aside from the flowers already considered, deal largely with leaves of which there is an infinite variety. Most shapes can best be copied from nature. As for the fantasy flowers, here a greater variety of design can be achieved by making leaves larger or smaller, and by using different papers and different colors. Since most leaves follow much the same design only a few will be described here.

Basically, one uses crisp or stiff papers. Most glossy or coated papers are stiff enough, but thin-colored bristol or similar papers are excellent for the purpose. It is usually practical to multiple-cut leaves (See page XIII) if the paper is thin enough.

Cut round leaves as in the illustration (a). Score on dotted lines. For serrated edges clip all the way around as indicated. Glue florists' wire to back of leaf. Be sure to cut wire long enough to include stem and piece for attachment to other stems (b). Rose leaves are made the same as above; follow illustration for special formation (c). Strap leaves (d). Wire as above (e). Follow illustration (e) for ferns.

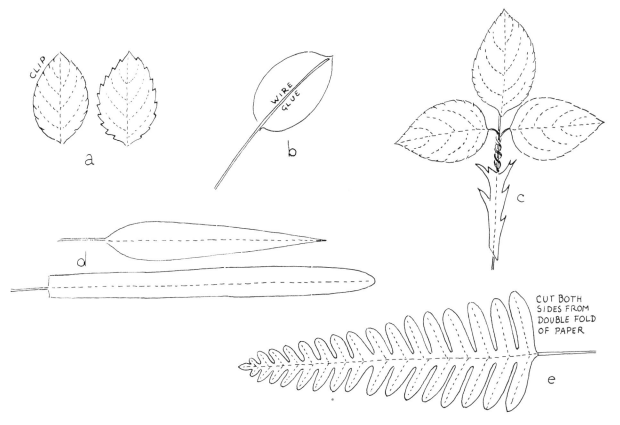

CUT BOTH
SIDES FROM
DOUBLE FOLD
OF PAPER

95

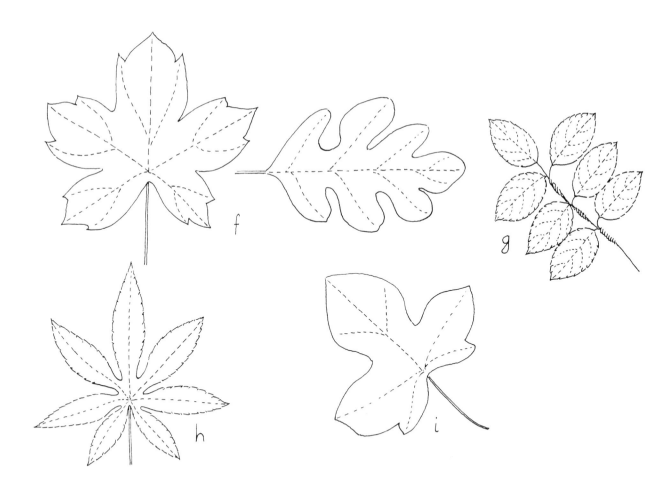

Maple and oak leaves (f) follow the same method. Composite leaves and such leaves as wild rose and Japanese maple (g and h) do, too. Use very thin wire for for backing the leaves. Twist wires together and use as stem. Odd-shaped leaves such as trilobe (i) are made in the same manner. Attach any of these leaves to main stems of flowers, plants, or trees by first attaching wire, and then covering joint with florists' tape or crepe paper "ribbon."

TINY PLANTS

A special kind of plant is made for doll-house gardens or garden models. Useful as a base for such plants are the caps of toothpaste tubes and similar tiny containers; these are transformed into flower pots and urns. They are filled with plasticene or other modeling clay, which also can serve as soil for the doll-house gardens.

To start with the stalk-type plants, make stalks of varying lengths (a). Make stems of cotton-covered wire. Make flowers by rolling "crumbs" out of snippets of tissue paper of various flower colors between thumb and fore-finger. They will be tiny, some a little larger than others. For leaves make little strips of paper backed by wire. Stick "crumbs" to wire, starting with

96

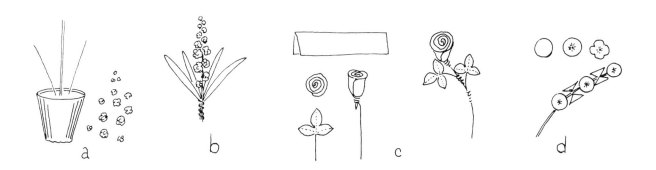

tiny ones at top and graduating the size as you work toward the bottom (b). Now combine leaves and flower stalk, and insert stalk into small container or in "flower bed."

Imagination has plenty of room for expression with these little plants. There can be unlimited variations on the one described above. For example, miniature roses may be made by folding, rolling, and twisting snippets of tissue paper (c). Build up plants with thin wire. Attach a rose to end of each branch. Add a few tiny leaves. Use glue sparingly. Make tiny flowers by pricking a hole in center of dot stickers (d) and glue to wire stem.

PLANT-LIKE DECORATIONS

For decorations to hang on wall or door, combine many fantasy flowers with leaves on wires. Use main stem of bamboo, dowel, or something similar to make bouquet-like structure (a). Or make main stem long enough so that it can stand in an appropriate container (b). Another variation may be a plant or topiary shrub, here using only one kind of leaf. For the topiary, use styrofoam ball on dowel (c). Variations can be made by using different colors or shades of a color on one plant. Flowers can be used, being attached in same way as leaves.

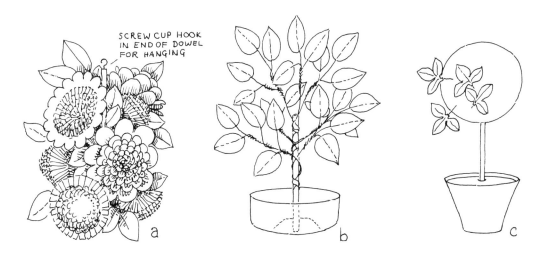

SCREW CUP HOOK
IN END OF DOWEL
FOR HANGING

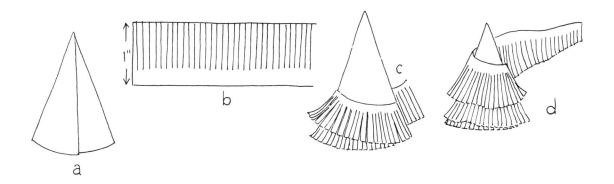

TREES

To design a coniferous tree, it is necessary to cut a cone (one-third circle) of dark green bristol board or poster board. White board painted green is just as acceptable. Glue edges together (a). Cut 1-inch-wide strips of green tissue paper. Cut ⅛ inch fringe (b). Wrap fringe around cone, and tack it with glue as you go around layer over layer. Let fringe edge gradually climb— about ⅛ inch or ¼ inch at each time around (c). Finish by cutting fringe off at an angle. Glue end down to point of cone (d).

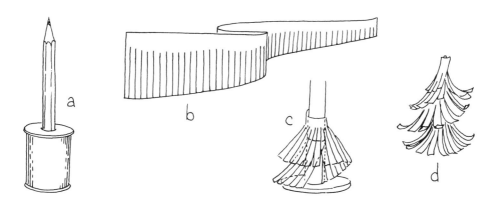

For another such tree, start with a spool emptied of its thread for the base. Cover middle part with a strip of bright paper. Take a stub of pencil, say 3 inches long, and insert into hole of spool (a). Cut a strip of stiff green paper, and cut fringe as in illustration (b). Using spots of glue, wind fringe around pencil, starting with widest end at the bottom (c). Climb about ¼ inch each round until narrowest end reaches the top. Clip off fringe, and secure well with glue (d). Curl up fringe ends by brushing upwards with hand.

Deciduous trees can be varied in many ways by making thicker or thinner, taller or shorter trunks, and by using the many different shapes for the crowns. Start by making a base so the tree can be moved around or plan to insert tree trunk in clay or plasticene ground of miniature garden. For base cut circle of cardboard and cover with green or brown tissue paper to be glued down securely all over (a). Make trunk out of brown poster or bristol board, rolling to a ¼-inch cylinder (b). Bend roots out to a 90 degree angle. Glue roots down to base, centering trunk (c).

For crown of tree, make many long shreds of green tissue paper (or use Easter basket green). Crumple them into a ball (or other shape tree crown). Affix to top of trunk, using glue (d). As crown is being shaped, drop bits of glue into mass of shreds. This will hold the pieces together, and once glue is dry, the crown will hold its shape. Patience is required here. Continue to shape while the glue is drying. Trim off stray long ends. Avoid using too much glue, and do not pack too tightly.

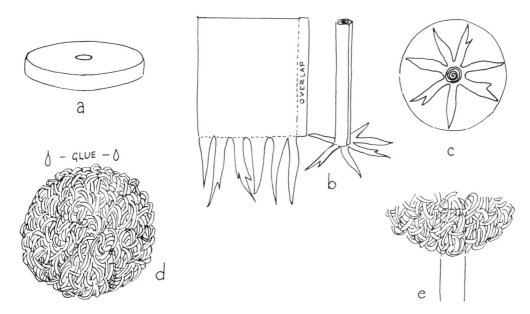

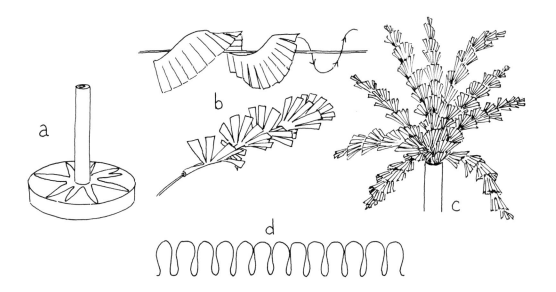

Branched trees call for a trunk similar to the deciduous, but a little shorter and narrower (a). Start by cutting pieces of wire for branches. Make long fringed "ribbon" of green crepe paper. Wrap "ribbon" around wire to give effect of leaves (b). Finish ends with bit of glue. When all branches are finished, secure them in trunk. Bend the branches out (c). For larger trees, cut "ribbon" of crepe paper with leaves (d). Otherwise handle in the same way as with the deciduous tree.

To create an *espalier* tree, secure a 12-inch-long piece of dowel (3/16 inch in diameter) and insert in a block of wood or styrofoam (round or square). With a knife, knotch the dowel at three evenly spaced points about 3 inches apart (a). Cut three wires for branches, and twist center of each wire firmly around a notch on dowel (b). Bring wires to other side of dowel, and twist firmly again. Bend wires out and up to form branches. Now wrap entire tree with crepe paper "ribbon" or florists' tape (c). Tree will now be decorated by winding fringe or leaf fringe (as in branched trees) and by attaching leaves and fruit and flowers. Artificial birds may also find a good perch here.

A miniature garden may well bring together all the skills involved in creating paper flowers, plants, and trees. (See doll houses and villages, Chapter 2.)

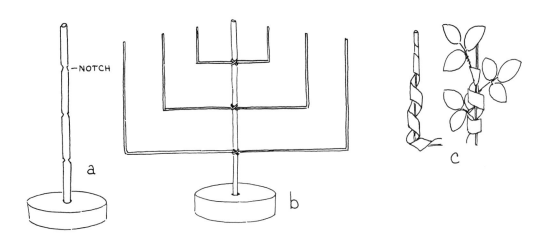

CHAPTER 7

DOLLS, ANIMALS, BIRDS AND FISH

Dolls are created by artists to look beautiful, especially to little girls. Dolls are also enjoyed by the mothers, who sometimes like to make them, this being an art that even with the most creative person, calls for some practical knowledge. In this special area of creativity, cut-out dolls provide an interesting beginning.

CUT-OUT DOLLS

First draw a figure on thin white cardboard, bristol or similar paper. Paint on features and possibly undergarments with water colors or felt markers. Cut out figure (a) and use its outline for outlines on thinner paper to base dresses on. Always supply dresses with tabs at crucial points to attach to the figure (b). The figure can be painted on both sides, and in that case two dresses (front and back) can be made (c).

Though cut-outs are usually made for little girls, they often serve a useful purpose as models for the designing of clothes. If you wish to get into this, cut a figure with proportions somewhat like your own. Sketch dresses, suits, and gowns, always following the figure outlines.

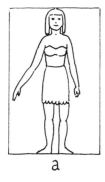
a

b

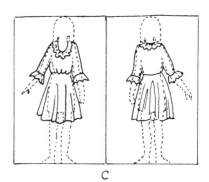
c

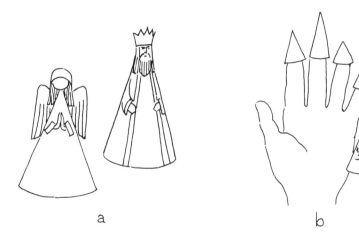

a   b

CONE DOLLS

These are far from the least important in doll design. They are by nature static, and so must be viewed in terms of their being display figures (a), for Christmas *creches* and the like. Versatile, tiny cone dolls make excellent finger puppets (b). The cones are cut as large as you wish.(See Page XIII).Each cone is topped with a commercial doll head made of cotton or papier-mâché or styrofoam. These heads come in many sizes(see Page 160). If small ones are not readily available, large wooden beads may be used. Decorate the dolls with cut-out accessories. Use paper fringe or crumpled, finely-snipped tissue paper for hair and beards. All kinds of paper may be used and can be supplemented with paper lace, embossed foil edging, and decorative floral stickers. Such a doll needs little more than wings to become a Christmas angel.

CYLINDRICAL DOLLS

Start by making a cylinder for the body and two for the arms. Attach arms by flattening one end of each, and gluing or stapling to upper end of body (a). Cut and make a smaller cylinder for the head, leaving a tab for connecting the head to the body (b). Your creative gift is given great leeway in decorating the figure, sparing no elaboration with fancy paper and other embellishments. Chinese dancing dolls are made this way, adding a fringe of bristles

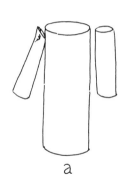

a

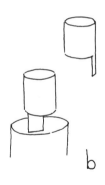

b

GLUE FRINGE
TO INSIDE
OF SKIRT

c

to the lower edge of the body cylinder (c). The artist is left to find bristles where he or she may: old brushes of many kinds or discarded false eyelashes. Finely-fringed foil paper will do if nothing better is available. Then comes decoration with colors, Oriental papers, or other flamboyance. When this creative work is done, the dolls are placed on any vibrating musical instrument—and they will dance.

CIRCULAR DOLLS

Draw a circle on thin vellum or bristol board. In the circle draw the figure, and color in any details with water color or ink or felt markers. Cut out and make notches as indicated (a). Hook the notches, and staple or glue.

To make a miniature ballet scene, the little dancers can be glued to a stage by their toes. They are, of course, quite small and if held in place until the glue sets, they will remain standing on their toes. An interesting alternative is to glue each dancer to a small disk or block so that they may be moved around (b).

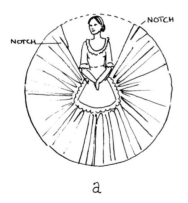

a

b

a

b

DANCING PAIR

Take an ordinary white business envelope. Fold it in half lengthwise, and draw a half figure on it as in illustration (a). Cut out the figure, and unfold. Color the figures on both sides, and open so they will hold each other up (b).

DOLL CHAINS

Fold a strip of paper of the proportions of about 10 by 2½ inches, in harmonica pleats so that there are 8 sides of paper (a). Sketch figures as shown. Cut out figures so that hands remain uncut on the folded edges. The first dancer's hand can be glued to the last dancer's hand to form a kind of "ring around the rosies (b)." Decorate the figures, and let them dance around a birthday cake. Pink elephants are as easily made, and provide an interesting variation. If you wish a wide ring, fold a longer strip in proportion to its width, and draw more than one figure, remembering to leave connecting pieces (c). This, too, is the technique for making garlands such as glorify many holiday occasions.

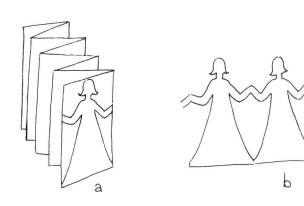

a

b

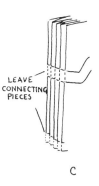

LEAVE CONNECTING PIECES

c

JUMPING JACKS AND MARIONETTES

Cut all the pieces shown in pattern (a) and with hole puncher make holes at the joints where indicated. Attach all joints with the smallest size envelope

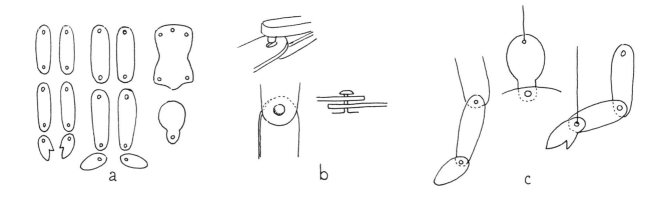

a   b   c

clips or clasps (b). The clips should not be bent close to the heads so that the joints will be very loose and movable. Then attach strings to head and ankle and wrist joints (c). This is, of course, the area of invention and excitement. You wonder first if it works, and then try to make it work.

PUPPETS

Make heads and hands of papier-mâché in much the same way as you would a whole head mask. (See masks and page 66). Make hands with plastic thimbles as base (a). Animal puppets can be made in a similar way. Make the body part of crepe paper, gathered and attached to the neck and wrist (b).

THIMBLE   a   USE A PIECE OF MAILING TUBE FOR NECK LINING   b

TWO-SIDED ANIMALS

Almost any four-legged animal can be simulated along basic lines. Using bristol board or other sturdy paper, draw two identical pieces as in pattern (a). Cut them out, and score on dotted line. Fold legs down, and glue the body pieces together at points indicated in pattern (b). Now the artist is free to paint and otherwise decorate the animal appropriately.

Many animals must be seen as decorative creatures, for example, the deer (1), cow (2), lamb (3), donkey (4), cat (7), dog (5), rabbit (6), and squirrel (8) to mention a few. All of these may be cut out of paper as previously indicated. The paper to be used must be stiff enough to support the animal or

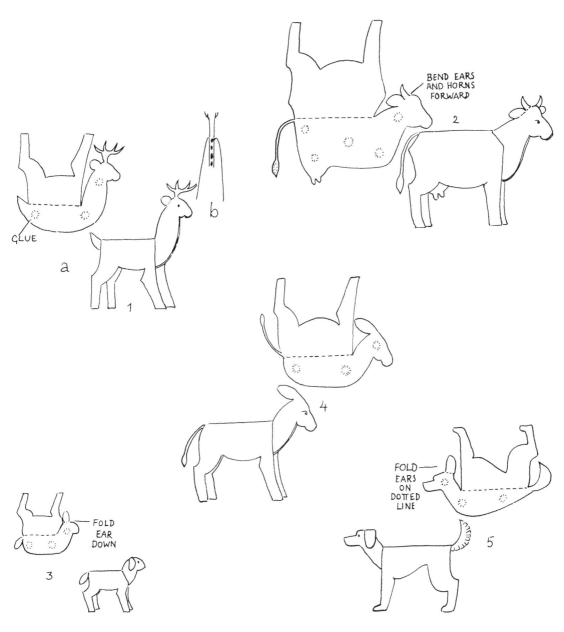

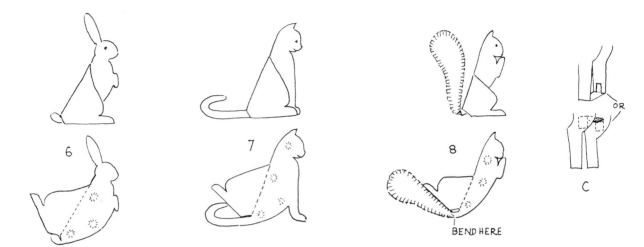

6   7   8   C

BEND HERE

be supplied with short supports between the feet. For this, cut narrow strips of the same paper, and bend a tab up at each end, and glue to both front legs and both hind legs (c).

CYLINDER ANIMALS

To create such animals out of paper, the artist should have a fairly good idea of the basic construction. One must go by the proportions because the details are obscured by the cylinder shapes, so it is mainly a case of fat and short and long and thin cylinders (a). Tops of the cylinders (of the legs, for example) can be cut off at an angle. Give the connecting edges a margin, enough to cut tabs for gluing (b), Use thin bristol or similar paper. Of course you will want to paint and decorate these animals, not forgetting paper saddles of gay colors (c).

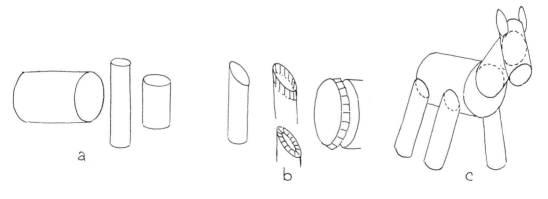

a   b   c

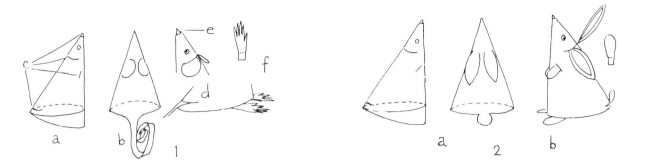

CONE ANIMALS

The cone shape is suitable especially for sitting animals of which most interesting is the mouse, closely followed by rabbits and squirrels.

For an utterly charming mouse (1), start by making a cone of ⅓ circle of gray paper. Cut off cone at angle as indicated (a). Make a second cone same as gray one of pink paper, cutting a long tail on edge as in pattern (b). Cut slot for ears in first cone, holes for eyes and second slot for tail, and small slots for front feet. Snip off nose (c). In pink cone cut two round ear flaps. Now put the pink cone inside the gray one. Put the ears through the slot in first cone and tail through the tail slot. Pink tip will show where

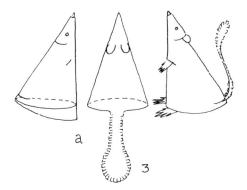

gray nose was snipped off (e). Draw eyes on pink cone. Curl tail. Cut 4 feet as in pattern of pink paper, and glue to inside of cone (f).

For the rabbit (2), make in the same way as the mouse, but use white paper. Use pink cut-outs for ear lining or use paint. Make a pink eye and nose. Cut pieces as in pattern (a). Bend ears up or down (b).

A squirrel calls for slightly different development. Cut two cones as for mouse, but cut smaller ears, and a very large tail (a). Draw eye. Use tan or brown paper for the outside cone, and a lighter shade inside. Make feet as for mouse.

CUT-OUT ANIMALS

Either draw an animal or use a sticker on a base of bristol board as in pattern (a). Cut out figure and base, and fold on dotted line (b). Make a support of bristol board. Cut a narrow strip long enough to reach from main part of body to base (at a 45 degree angle) plus small tabs at each end (c) cut out of bristol board. Glue in place. Cut-out animals can also be glued as ornaments to boxes or baskets (d).

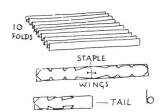
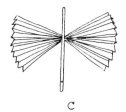

a

10 FOLDS

STAPLE

WINGS

TAIL b

c

BIRD BODY

GLUE OR STAPLE HERE

d

BIRDS OF A FEATHER

To make a dove with pleated wings and tail, cut a piece of white cardboard, illustration board, or heavy bristol board in the shape of the body of the dove (a). For color, cover with foil or bright-colored paper on both sides. Cut a notch in the back as indicated. Make the wings by folding a rectangular piece of tissue paper or other thin paper into accordion pleats, and cutting small pieces out of edges (b). Staple the wings in the center, and fan out the sides (c). Place in notch of body. Make a tail much like the wings, making only one fan (d). Glue or staple tail to body.

PEACOCK WITH PLEATED WINGS AND TAIL

Cut body of peacock-colored board as in pattern (a) or cover a piece of board with colored paper. Make a slot in body as indicated. The wings will be made as for the dove, carefully working the folded wing section through the body slot (b). Unfolding the wings and bringing them together over the back, glue or staple them together (c). Make a tail as for dove, but slightly larger (d). The "eyes" on the tail may be decorated with brightly-colored pieces of paper before being attached to body with glue or staples.

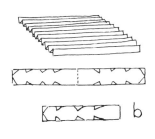
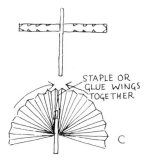

a

b

STAPLE OR GLUE WINGS TOGETHER

c

d

TRIANGULAR BIRD (THE WREN)

Cut a piece of tan or brown paper as in pattern (a). All the triangles are equal in size. Cut a tail and wing of the same paper (b). Draw feathers on the wings and tail in color. Draw an eye on each side of one point (c). Attach tail and wings with glue (d) and make feet of board (e) with sharp knife. Split board, and glue body to feet. Make a beak at top of front triangle.

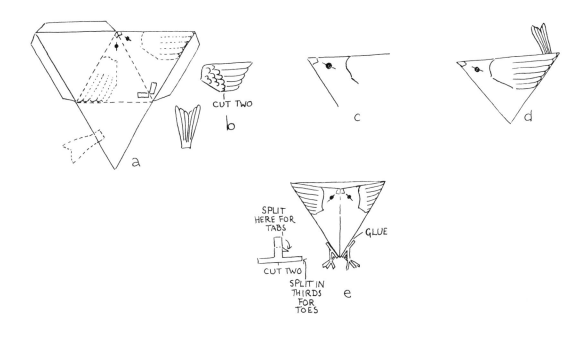

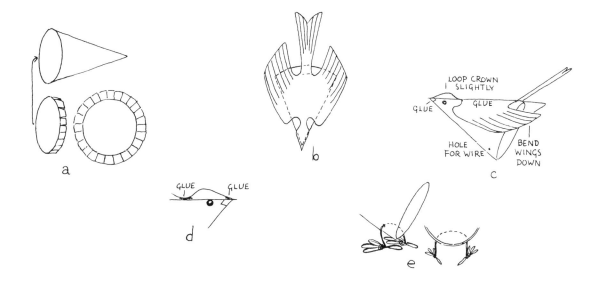

CONE BIRD

Make a one-third circle cone of crisp paper. Glue a bottom of same color to the cone (a). Cut a tail-wing crown-piece as in pattern, of a contrasting color (b). Glue tail-wing crown-piece to seam of cone from crown to point (c). Draw on details such as eyes and beak (d). Make wire feet. Put wire body first, and bend wire to form feet (e).

PLUMES

These are important to all birds, natural and artificial. For the latter, start by cutting a double fringe out of at least four layers of tissue paper and of the length of the plume (a). Mount wire in middle of fringe (b) and

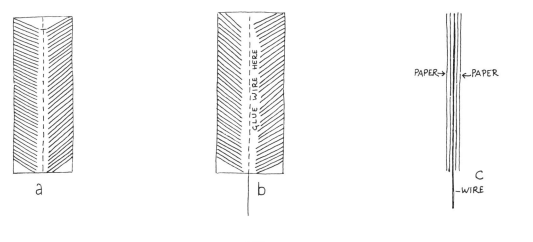

glue other layers to both sides of wire (c). Cut fringes at an angle to wire (d) to produce a feather shape. Curl ends of fringe (e).

PEACOCK FEATHERS

These are cut very narrow to a long double fringe (a). Glue to wire. Make eye as shown in illustration (b). Glue to end of wire and fringe (c). Use peacock colors and foil papers, which come in shades of blue, blue-green, green, and others.

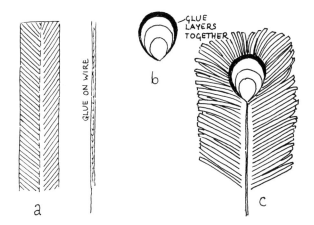

FISHES

As with the birds, you start with the cone. Begin by drawing two circles of the same size. Draw the gills, lips, fins, and tails as in pattern (a). If you are using a paper with color on only one side, be sure to reverse the features. Then cut out the fish in one piece; cut gills, and glue them to body as indicated (b). Glue fins together. Put just a spot of glue on the lips, and glue them together. Decorate in any way you wish. All the possibilities are there, such as making a group in different sizes and colors to make an exciting mobile. Fish seem to respond interestingly when hung by the back fin.

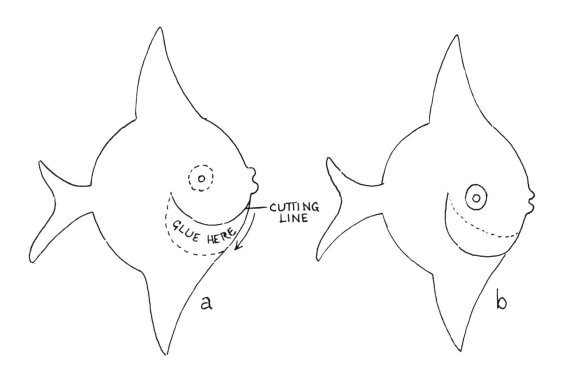

CUTTING LINE

GLUE HERE

a

CUTTING LINE

b

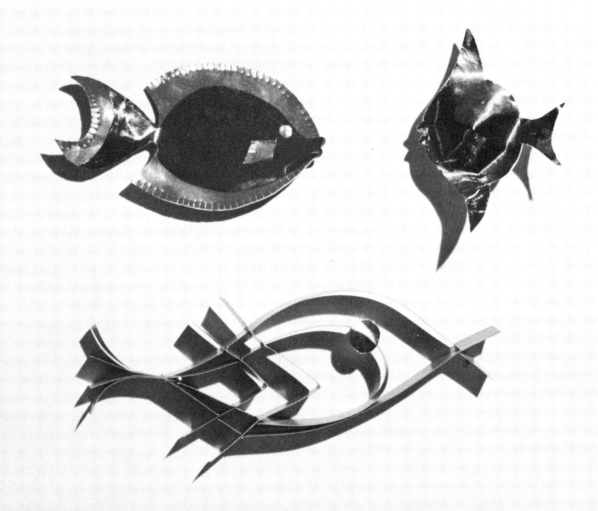

For a second fish you begin by cutting strips of paper ½ inch wide (plus or minus for the whales and the minnows), and get guidance from the pattern for the structural members (a) such as the two pieces needed for the outside lines, one looped piece for the inside line, and two folded pieces for the fins. Notch all the pieces as indicated (b) and hook them together, gluing eyes to looped strip.

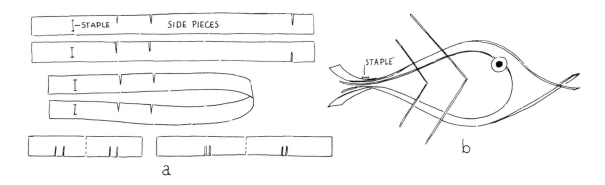

For still another fish start by cutting from a rather stiff bright blue paper. Snip the edge where indicated (a). Then cut two side pieces as in pattern (b) using navy blue or black. Score on dotted lines, and cut fin. Draw an eye or use a cut-out. Put a thin line of glue around all edges of side pieces, and glue to main piece. The choice of colors is up to the artist though gold and silver might be good choices for fish.

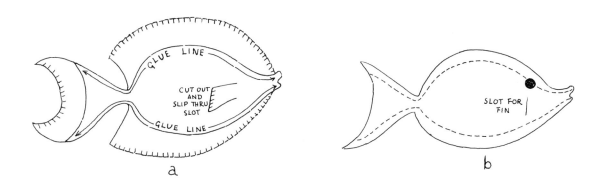

CHAPTER 8
ORIGAMI AND MOBILES

Among all the arts that have come to America from the East, the one called origami holds high place. The name is Japanese. At its best the art calls upon many artistic skills such as draughtsmanship, feeling for color, knowledge of sculpture, and the understanding to bring all of these together in artistic expression.

If the creation of origami sounds outside the reach of the aspiring artist, this impression fades usually once the paper and scissors are in hand. You, whether artist or neophyte, take a firm grip on your talent and understanding, and attack the problem, perhaps that of creating a colorful feline standing on its own legs in three dimensions, or perhaps a fantasy flower, or another-world lantern shade—or whatever your imagination encourages you to attempt. The new artist is often surprised to discover how much talent he has.

Origami is an art, and once the admirer has copied other people's work for a while, he is full of desire to set forth under his own adventurous sails. Such adventurous sailing would reasonably involve spin-offs from early trials with folding squares of paper. Any colorful, easily foldable paper is suitable, but Japanese paper intended for this purpose is available almost everywhere, and usually pre-cut in squares ready to use.

Many shapes can be folded from each square, and all kinds of objects and animals and flowers magically appear by folding each square diagonally, and then across. Then pull out a point here and tuck in a point there, and finally it all seems very simple.

A FLYING CRANE

Take a perfect square of paper, and fold it diagonally twice (a). Bring point B over to point C (b). Then bring D to C. Turn paper over, and bring A to D (c). Fold A and D up to top point (d) and fold on dotted lines toward center (on both sides) (e). Pull A and D upward and refold (f). Fold on dotted lines (g) (both sides) and bring points B and C out, and up to A and

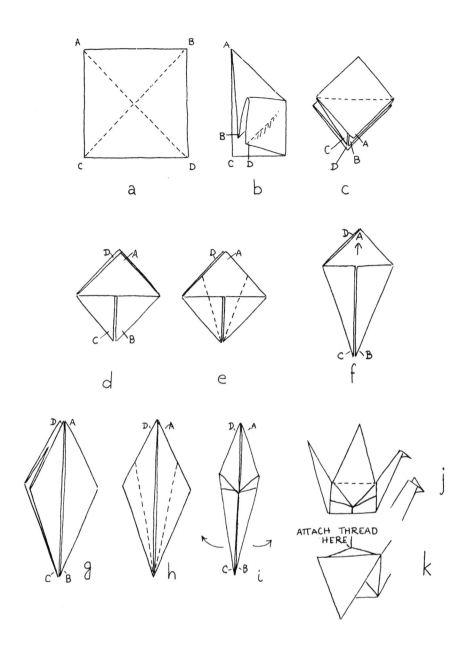

D (h). Finish the crane by folding wings (A and D) down, and bend head B down. Bring the tail (C) down just a bit (i). Hang crane from string or wire put through the back (j). Make a flock of these cranes, and hang them as mobiles or on Christmas trees.

A DOVE

Start with a square of paper. Fold it in half crosswise, and then again (a) and fold the resulting four squares each in half diagonally (b). Fold two corners of one half on dotted lines (c) and fold the paper in half (d). Reverse

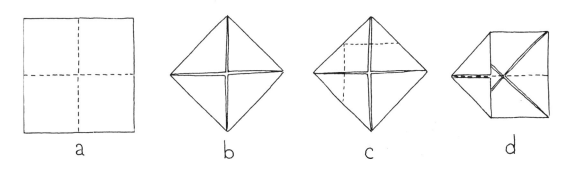

a   b   c   d

119

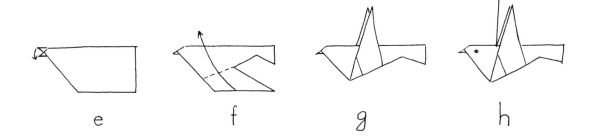

fold the tip on dotted line (e). Cut out a piece as indicated for tail and wing (f). Fold up wings on dotted line (g). Draw an eye on each side, and hang by thread through back (h).

A FROG

Start by folding a square of paper in half crosswise twice (a). Bring corners to the center by folding each of four squares diagonally (b). Bring the two side corners to the center (c). Fold the third corner back and to the center (d). Fold remaining corner on dotted lines, and fold tip under (e). Fold A and B under on dotted line (f). Cut fore feet and hind feet and eyes, and glue them to body as indicated (g). Draw on other details such as nostrils.

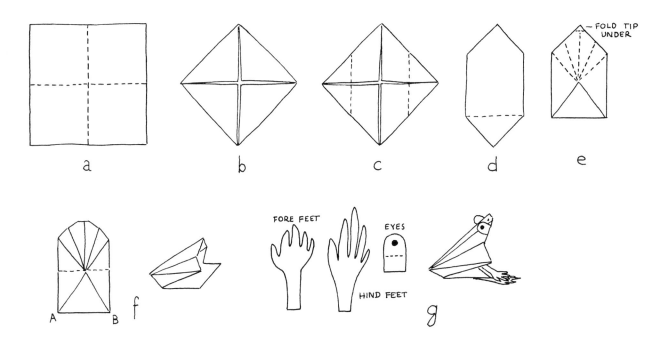

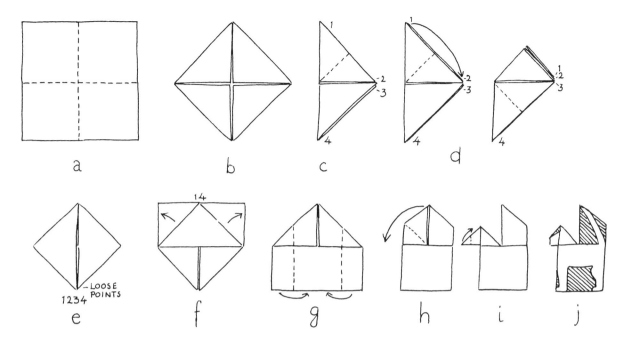

a   b   c   d

e   f   g   h   i   j

A CAT OR TIGER

Cut a square of striped or marbleized paper. Fold it in half crosswise twice (a). Bring corners to center (b). Fold resulting square in half diagonally (c). Bring top point down between two side points (d). Bring bottom point up between two side points. Turn paper so that openings run vertically (e) and connected point is up and the loose points down. Fold bottom point up to top point (f) and do the same with the other bottom point. Turn paper around so point is up (g). Fold on dotted lines toward inside center, and then fold other side (h). Fold left top point down, and fold inward on dotted line (i). Fold tip back inward on dotted line. Now cut out figure as in illustration (j). Draw in eyes and other details.

A POODLE

Fold the same way as for cat, but cut out figure according to pattern (a). Use black paper. The same goes for a Schnauzer, using gray paper, cutting as in illustration (b).

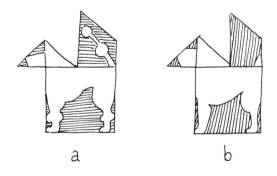

a   b

Mobile is a comparatively new name in the arts, and it matters not how you try to relate it to the others, whether as a painting in motion, a sculpture in motion, or even Aeolian poetry, the mobile will in the end be accepted as its own form of art expression.

More than any other art form, the mobile appeals to people of all ages. A baby is comforted and no doubt charmed to look up from the cradle at a flock of artificial birds on the wing. Grown-ups find that a mobile counteracts the tendency to rigidity in room construction and furniture design, and for parties presents art in a light way that adds a sparkle to the frivolity. The elderly find the gentle, sometimes almost imperceptible motion, easeful.

The mobile as an art form will take its place with the rest very largely because of the work of Alexander Calder, a third-generation sculptor who revealed his fascination with art in motion in a Paris exhibition in 1932. Since then Calder's mobiles have been admired in most of the art centers of the world.

If this sounds formidable, the fact is that anybody can make a mobile, and no one should be discouraged by the thought of failure to match Calder, nor by initial difficulties. (Perhaps Calder's early mobiles did not work out very well.) As he may have, you cut and try, and cut and try again.

Of the many ways to make mobiles, some of the simplest are among the most charming. After deciding on the design, the problem becomes one of balance. The parts must swing free of each other, that is, each branch of the mobile will be on a different level of balance relative to the main branch. However, if two or more branches hang from the main branch at the same level, the main branch should extend far enough so that the other branches (and objects) will still swing free and be balanced. Trial and error are involved, and experimenting with a view to developing a well-balanced mobile.

You do best to begin with the lowest branch or branches. Use copper wire for the branches because it is easy to bend and form. Black cotton thread may be used for the joints where required. It is the least visible of threads. Design your mobile with straight or bent branches according to your inclination. Again the number of ornaments that may be made to hang on the mobile is not fixed. It will suffice here to outline a few designs for the structure and for a few of the ornaments. Then the innovator and artist must take over (a, b and c).

REGULAR

a

IRREGULAR

b

c

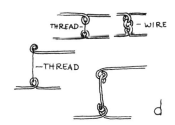

STRAIGHT BEAMS OR BRANCHES

First make the objects you are going to hang on the mobile so that they will be ready when your framework is built. Many ideas will be found in Chapter 7, as well as in the descriptions of the stars and angels in Chapter 12.

Follow pattern (a or b) but keep in mind that each step is not finished until the balance has been found. Make small loops at the end of each branch (d) so that threads can be attached to them. Tie thread to branches, adding a touch of glue when balance has been found.

Bent Beams Or Branches (c). Follow instructions for first mobile.

CIRCULAR GO-ROUND

Make several sizes of one kind of bird (a). (See origami for ideas.) Make a ring of wire or rattan. Splice the rattan or twist the wire to fasten ends. Take several lengths of thread (as many as the number of birds). Metallic thread or colored threads are suitable. Make a knot at the end of each. Hang each bird from the ring at a different height (b). Secure all the threads with a knot. Now bring the free ends of the threads together in a knot, making adjustments so that the ring hangs level. Tie a loop knot in the thread ends and hang up the finished mobile.

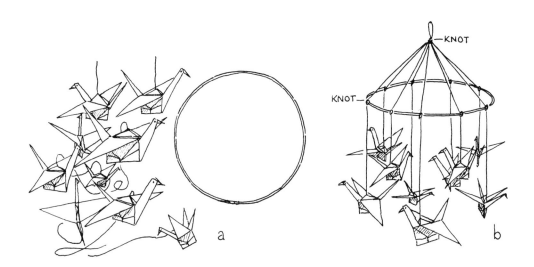

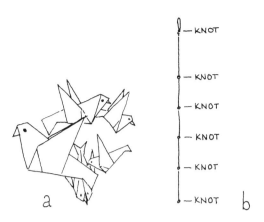

a

—KNOT
—KNOT
—KNOT
—KNOT
—KNOT
—KNOT

b

STRING MOBILE

Make five different sizes of one kind of bird (a). Tie a knot at one end of thread, then cut the thread long enough to go through all the birds, allowing for a space between one bird and another, and sufficient extra thread to hang it by (b). Make the knot large enough to keep it from slipping through the hanging hole in the birds. Thread the birds on one by one, tying a knot under each before going on to the next. Tie a loop knot at the end of the string.

INDIAN CHILD'S MOBILE

Make twelve discs the same size of many colors of paper (a). Glue them together two by two. Make ten birds of many colors. Follow illustrations to make pattern pieces for the bird (b). Cut one piece each of cardboard, and trace ten copies of each of the bodies on thick paper, the wing tail pieces on tissue paper. Twist the wing tail pieces as shown, and place them between body parts before you glue tabs to the indicated points. Glue heads together (c).

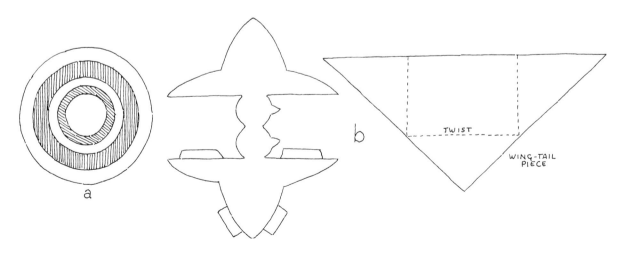

a

b

TWIST

WING-TAIL PIECE

Starting at the bottom, string a thread through a bird and the other end to bottom edge of one disc. Follow pattern for further stringing of mobile. Finish by tying strings to stick or dowel (d).

C

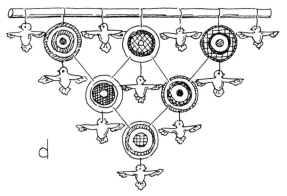

d

DANISH STAR MOBILE

Such a mobile is best made with real straw and paper though it may also be made with soda straws. With six straws make a 6-pointed star (a). With 3 straws (6 half straws)make such a star of smaller size.

Tie all joints with bright-colored embroidery thread (b). Using the same thread, tie seven small stars to the end of the same number of threads (c). Make small star as described in (b). The length of each thread is subject to design considerations (each about a yard long should suffice). Having cut many short pieces of straw—about ½ inch in length—then cut many little double squares of brightly colored paper (d).

Thread a darning needle with a knot at one end to pick up one of the stars. Then thread a piece of straw, and alternate straw and paper until the creation reaches 3 inches. The next step is simple because it only involves duplicating the foregoing 5 times over (e).

The key to success is the seventh thread which will reach all the way to the top of the mobile, hanging free. Now attach threads to points of smaller star. Tie knots there, and continue threading paper squares and straw pieces for 4 inches. Then tie points of larger star (f) and attach new threads to center joints of large star. Apply the paper squares and straw pieces within a 7-inch area. Join all seven threads together and tie into a very secure knot. Use one of the threads to continue on for 3 or 4 inches with paper squares and straw. Use a loop-knot for hanging the mobile.

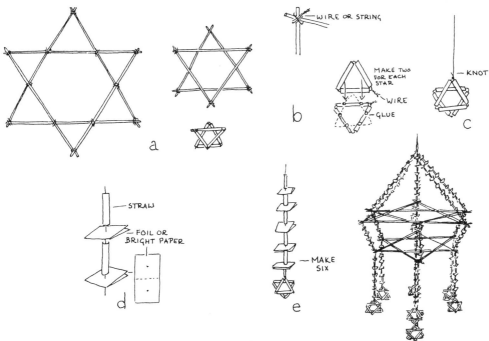

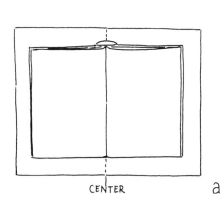

CENTER

a

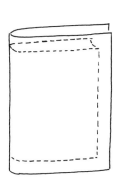

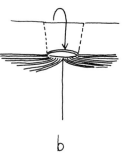

b

CHAPTER 9

DUST JACKETS, RUFFS.
PLACE MATS, CACHEPOTS
AND DESK ACCESSORIES

This chapter deals particularly with the artistic treatment of what might be considered mundane things: dust jackets for books, meat ruffs; other kitchen decorations, such as place mats woven of plastic-coated paper and metallic paper; and *cachepots* to cover flower pots.

DUST JACKETS

Choose a suitable paper from the gift-wrap patterns—from the coated patterns to the foil papers. Some of these have plastic coating, which makes them suitable for cookbook jackets or for the covering of children's books.

Begin by placing the book on the wrong side of paper that is the size to go around the back and cover both covers, with an overlap of at least 2 inches at each end and an overlap at the top and bottom (a). Determine the center, and place the book back on the center line. Cut at a slight angle on the dotted lines, and turn and fold resulting flap to inside of jacket (b). Fold overlaps to inside of book cover, and fold corners under as indicated (c). The top and bottom overlaps are tucked to the outside of the book cover (d). Decorate the finished cover with initials or personal motifs by cutting them out of contrasting paper labels, and gluing them to jacket. Or design your own.

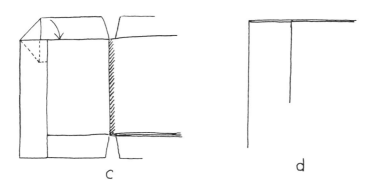

c

d

MEAT RUFFS

These are used for chops, crown roast, or poultry. The paper should be rather crisp, such as bond or a paper slightly heavier than bond. A shiny white freezer paper is suitable. These ruffs can be made in advance, but the size of the bone it will cover should be kept in mind. Cut a strip of paper, and fold it in half lengthwise (a). Cut any of the fringes suggested, the

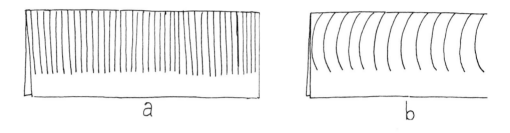

a   b

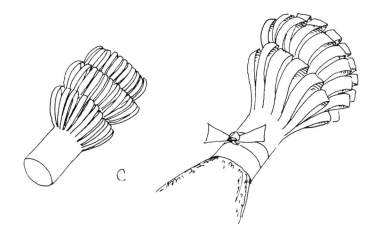

C

rounded ones with nail scissors (b). Unfold, and fold inside out. Wrap around leg ends of poultry, and glue in place or tie a narrow ribbon around it (c).

DOILIES AND CAKE RUFFS

For the decoration of cake, cookie, and candy dishes. Cut doilies of crisp white paper thin enough for the cutting through of several layers. Use a paper such as bond though foil paper and coated papers in colors are also suitable. Tissue paper can be used for dry cookies and candies, but probably not for cakes since they might cause the tissue paper to disintegrate and absorb their color.

For a round doilie, cut a circle of paper. Fold it in half, and again in half. Fold each quarter in half, and then fold the whole piece in half (a). Now cut out your design at random or according to a previously drawn design (b). Be careful to leave connecting strips in the design. If the cutting through many layers is difficult, mark important points with an awl or darning needle or ice pick. Then follow the design, cutting through a few layers at a time from point to point, and then through a few more until the cut-out is complete (c). Use the awl to add interest to your design.

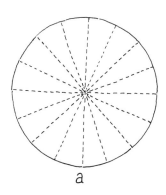

a

b

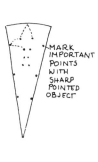

MARK IMPORTANT POINTS WITH SHARP POINTED OBJECT

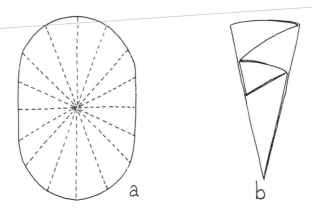

For an oval doilie, cut an oval out of one of the papers, and fold in half diagonally. Then fold the shorter portion in half, and the longer portion in half in the opposite direction (a). Cut the design similar to the design for the round doilie. Do not cut through outer edge (b).

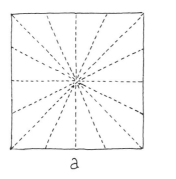

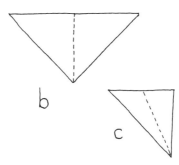

a

For a square doilie, start by cutting a square of paper, and folding it in half diagonally, and again in half (a). Then fold loose points in opposite directions (b). Fold piece in half again in two directions (c) and cut a design as for round doilie.

For cake ruffs, first pleat a strip of paper about five times the diameter of the cake in length and 2 or 3 inches wide. Mark off ½-inch pleats on wrong side of paper, and pleat (score first if paper is thick). Run a thread, string, or ribbon through holes punched 1-inch from the inner edge. Fit around cake, and tie in place.

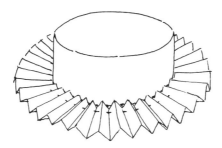

PLACE MATS

Cut oblongs of interesting papers. Without folding the center, bring the two ends together, and fold in half (a). In cutting the design, leave a margin of about ¾-inch (b). Unfold.

a

b

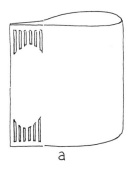
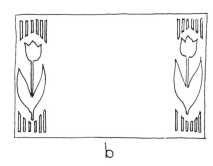

a   b

For another kind of place mat, cut rectangles of paper, the coated papers being especially suitable. Without making folds in the paper, cut simple edging or corner decorations (a). Cut contrasting figures or flowers, and apply them to the sides of the place mat (b). One or both sides of the place mat may be so decorated.

Still another place mat is made of two colors of coated paper. Cut a rectangle of the size you want of the first paper. Make the size easy to divide into squares in both directions (¾ inch by ¾ inch, or one by one). Mark off the width of the squares on the wrong side of the paper, and cut on the dotted lines (a). Using the second color, cut strips that are the width of the squares and as long as the whole mat (b). Weave each strip through the mat, and tack with glue on the back of the mat ends (c). The smaller the squares and the narrower the strips, the more intricate the weaving patterns you can make. Also, with finer weaving, it is possible to use more colors.

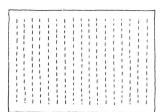
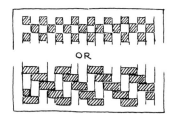

OR

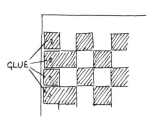

GLUE

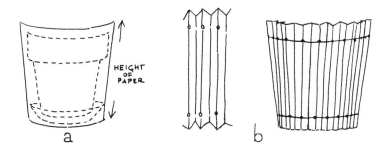

CACHEPOTS

As suggested by the French expression, these are used to hide pots although it might be more apropos to say they are used to decorate them. Whichever, glamorize flower pots with a pleated or cylinder-shaped *cache*. To make a pleated *cachepot* take a piece of paper of any color with pleating quality, not forgetting foil paper. The length of the strip of paper should be 5 times the diameter of the widest part of the flower pot or the saucer in which it stands (this will be covered, too). The width of the strip will be equal to the height of the pot, plus the height of the saucer and at least one extra inch (a). Mark ¾-inch pleats on wrong side of paper. If it seems necessary, score paper before folding the pleats, and notch each pleat at 1 inch from both edges with a hole puncher. Tie a string or ribbon around *cachepot* over all the holes (b) at two levels.

CYLINDER CACHEPOT

This is a cylinder made of bristol board or a similar paper, and used especially for flower pots to try to bring them up to the aesthetic level of their contents. It can be done, perhaps, by cutting a length that will fit loosely around the widest part of the flower pot, plus an overlap of ½ inch for gluing or stapling. The height will be the same as that of the flower pot, plus the height of the saucer and about 1 inch more to reach above the flower pot (a). Decorate as you wish.

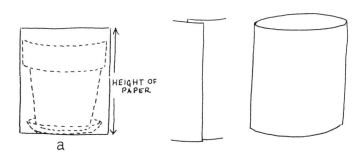

LABELS

Cut a pattern piece of cardboard in the shape of the labels you have in mind (a). Trace on the wrong side of paper, and cut out. Decorate and letter the labels before sticking them to jars or boxes. Make use of gummed paper if convenient, and perhaps add foil or flower stickers.

DESK SET

This includes a blotter, a container for pens and pencils, a stamp box, a note pad—all of which may be covered with attractive paper.

For the blotter, cut a piece of double-thickness cardboard; whatever the proportions, make sure that the corners are square. With a fancy paper such as one of the gift wraps, make two corner pieces and a strip along

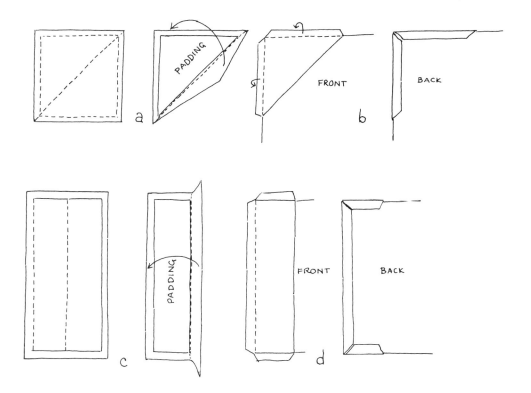

one side. Make the corner pieces by cutting two squares. Fold them in half diagonally. Put a triangle of padding such as kleenex or paper towels between the layers of paper (a) and glue on the backside of cardboard (b). Make the side strip about 3 inches wide. Cut a strip 6 inches wide plus overlap. The length is the same as board plus overlap at both ends. Fold strip in half and put padding between the layers of paper (c). Fold margins to the back, and glue them down (d). Now glue down a sheet of the same decorative paper to the back of the board following pattern (e). Cut a piece of blotting paper the size of the board, and tuck one short side under the side piece first and then the opposite corners under the corner pieces (f). It may be necessary to trim the blotter to make a good fit.

For the pencils-and-pens holder cut a piece of paper of the same kind

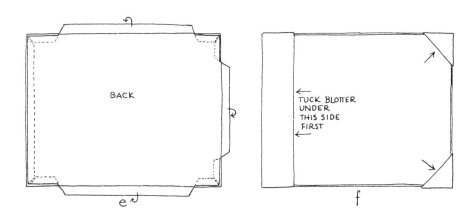

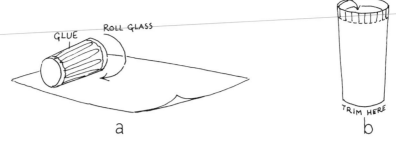

a   b

used for the blotter. Cover a glass with glue, roll it over the wrong side of the paper (a). Give end a ½-inch margin. Trim and glue to make a neat seam. Trim the lower edge, and glue any loose spots. Trim the top half inch from rim of glass. Apply glue to rim, and turn paper to inside of glass (b).

To make a three-drawer stamp box, follow the instructions for chest of drawers for doll house, page 31. Use the same paper as for the other items of the desk set.

For note pad, take two equal rectangles of 2-ply cardboard (the size depending upon the wish of the person who will use it, and to a lesser degree on the size of the desk). Make a hinge of 1-inch-wide Mystik tape, taping the outside first, and leaving a narrow margin on both ends. Fold over margins to inside. Stick more tape to inside, and trim edges (a). With the same tape make a pencil loop, sticking a piece of tape to itself in such a way as to leave room for the insertion of a pencil and remembering to leave a half inch at both ends for the tacking down (b). Now run a piece of tape across both ends.

To cover this note pad, cut out two pieces of equal size, not forgetting to leave a ½-inch margin on three sides of each piece. Place the covers on the wrong side of the pieces of paper, and glue the paper to the covers. Fold margins over and glue them to inside. Cut two equal pieces of paper for liners slightly smaller than the covers. Glue in place. Cut one more piece of the size of the liners, and fold in half. Glue this to lower edge of one side, forming a pocket to accommodate the back of note pad (d). Glue down all possible loose corners or edges.

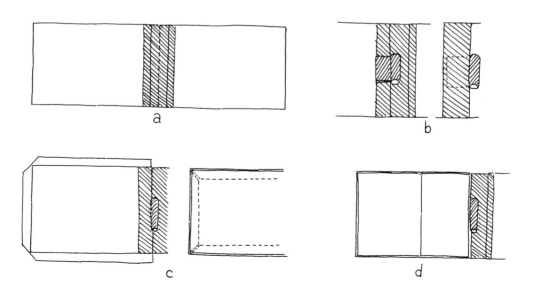

a   b

c   d

CHAPTER 10

VALENTINES, GREETING CARDS, BOOK MARKS AND FANS

Celebrations of one kind or another call forth the card, whether it is a calling card, a birthday card, a national holiday card, a Thanksgiving card, or a Christmas card, and though the commercial cards serve a noble purpose, there remains the possibility of creating your own greeting cards.

Sentiment exists on many levels, as the commercial greeting card people know, but its original purpose had to do with the billing and cooing of a male and female perhaps several millennia ago. Comparatively recently, such lovers were given their own special saint.

WOVEN HEART

Cut two pieces of paper as in pattern (a). Use two colors of paper, and cut even strips by cutting the dotted lines. Weave the strips together starting at the center of the heart (b). When the heart is finished, it can serve as a lovely envelope for a *billet-doux* or a hankie for your valentine.

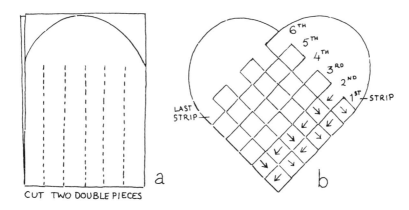

CUT TWO DOUBLE PIECES

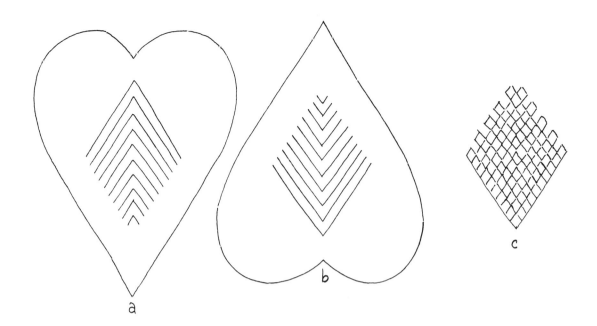

DOUBLE-HEART

In much the same way it is possible to weave two hearts together. First cut two hearts and fold them in half. Then cut strips at an angle as in pattern (a). The two hearts can be cut at the same time. Starting with the last strip of either heart, begin the weaving with the last strip of the other heart (b). Then weave strip after strip until all are used up (c). It is advisable to make a sample or two of waste paper to develop a little skill in the weaving.

HEART AND HAND

Cut one heart and one hand of two colors of paper (a). Fold both in half, and cut strips at an angle as in illustration. The strips should run in opposite directions. Weave in same way as the double heart (b). Decorate with floral stickers or foil or lace trimmings.

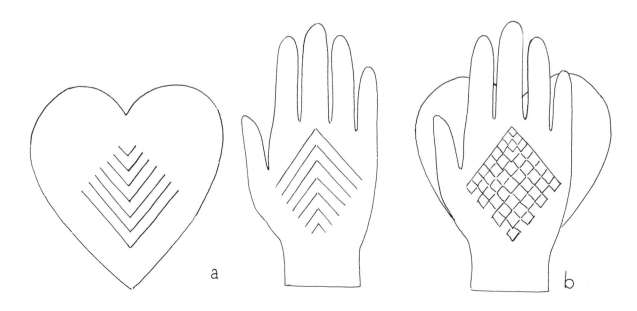

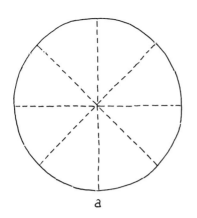
a

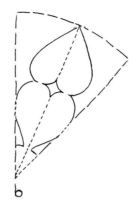
b

c

RING OF HEARTS

Fold a circle of paper (white is good for this valentine) in half four times (a). Cut the design as indicated (b). This will give a circle of eight hearts with a ring of eight hearts around them. Decorate each heart with pen and ink or felt markers, writing a little slogan or a poetic or personal phrase in each one (c).

LACE CUT-OUT

Fold a square of thin white paper (not tissue) such as onion skin. Fold paper in half three times, and sketch an interesting, possibly intricate design on one side of folded paper (a) and cut it out with cuticle scissors or other scissors fine enough to make tiny fringe edges, circles, and sharp corners. The finer the cut-out, the lacier the final result. The solid pieces offer an opportunity to write sweet messages (b). Tack the cut-out with white glue to a solid colored piece of paper to show up the delicacy of the valentine. Use extreme care when unfolding and flattening the cut-out to avoid breaking the connecting pieces.

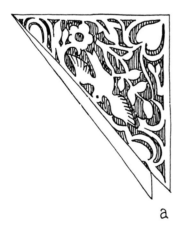
a

LACE AND STICKER JUMP-UPS

Use commercial valentine lace frames, or cut lace frames of crisp paper. Cut a lace frame as you would an oblong doilie, leaving an opening large enough to suit the design. Attach the frame to the card, with a floral sticker in the center, by making jump-ups. To make these, cut strips of tough, not too thick paper. Fold to form a spring with tab at each end for glue (a). Glue one jump-up under each corner of frame, one tab to lace, one to card (b). Decorate with little hearts and floral stickers.

OPEN-OUT VALENTINE

Fold a piece of drawing paper in half crosswise, and then again (a). With the folded edges to the left and at the bottom, decorate the front with paper lace and stickers or cut-outs (b). Then open the card, fold as in pattern (c) and cut out heart, trimming off excess paper. There is plenty of space for a message below. Color the heart red with paint or paper. Add decorations at your whim, perhaps to match the front. Now fold the card closed as indicated. The heart will fold up and out when opened (d).

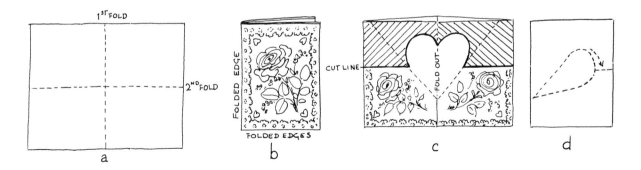

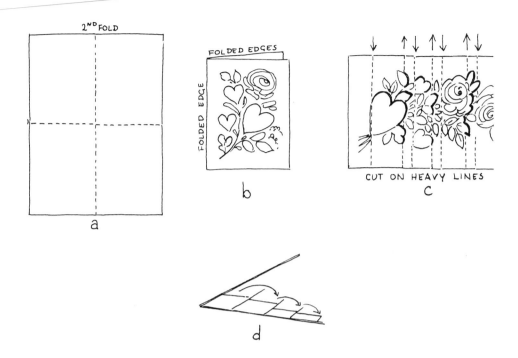

POP-UP VALENTINE

This is a simple but spectacular card. Take a piece of drawing paper, fold in half crosswise, and fold in half again (a). With the folded edges to the left and at the top, decorate the front with drawings of hearts and flowers (b). Open the card, and use the same motifs inside, covering the whole center of the spread (c). Make careful and barely visible marks in parallel vertical lines to show where the folds are to be made, considering your artistic design in determining where to place them. Now cut out the continuation of each motif on the top of the folds. Fold the card closed, and the hearts and flowers will pop out when the card is opened (d).

GREETING CARDS

Cards for any occasion can be made in somewhat the same way as the valentines, replacing the hearts and flowers with appropriate symbols.

Christmas Cards can be made individually if your list is not too long. Otherwise they can be hand-printed with a linoleum cut or potato print. Small stickers such as stars and dots can be added after printing. Start with colored paper, print with opaque paint, and add a few details with pen or brush. An interesting Christmas card can be created by combining a linoleum print and pop-up (See above description and illustration of pop-up Valentine.)

144

BOOK MARKS

These can be made using one or two layers of paper, but no more than that. Use one layer of opaque paper, and one of fairly transparent paper. Unless one has an especially large or small book in mind, six to ten inches would be a reasonable size. Start by cutting out a design of one piece of paper, having drawn the design lightly on one side with pencil. Cuticle scissors may be best for this purpose. Another way to make a book mark is to cut out a symmetrical design in thin paper. Start by folding a strip of paper lengthwise. Then cut your design (a). Unfold, and stick the thin paper to an opaque background strip (b).

a   b

145

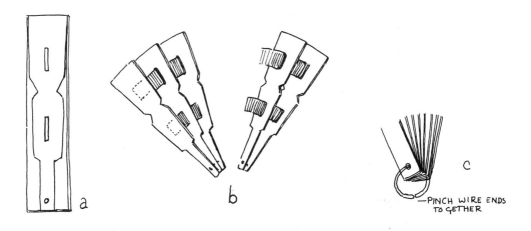

a

b

c

—PINCH WIRE ENDS
TO GETHER

SEPARATE SEGMENT FAN

Cut a dozen pieces of illustration board (double-sided, lightweight thickness) of the shape shown in pattern. Make slots where indicated—not in two end pieces. Make hole in stem with an awl (a). Attach narrow ribbon to one end piece, and run through all the pieces, fastening the ribbon to the other end piece (b). The ribbon should permit the pieces to overlap just a trifle. Run a piece of thick wire through stem holes. Clip wire, and pinch ends together (c). Decorate the individual segments before putting the ribbon through the slots with stickers, cut-outs, or paint.

JAPANESE FAN

Draw a half circle on foldable thick paper such as bristol board. About two-thirds of the way from outer edge to center, draw a second half circle (a). Divide smaller half circle into 12 equal parts, and then those equal parts in half. In doing this, mark only on the wrong side of paper. From center, draw through each mark a radius to outer edge. Cut on the line of the half circle. Score on radius lines, and fold accordion pleats (b). Split bamboo strips ¼ inch in width are the best for finishing this fan. If bamboo is not easily available, thin board strips will serve. Whichever

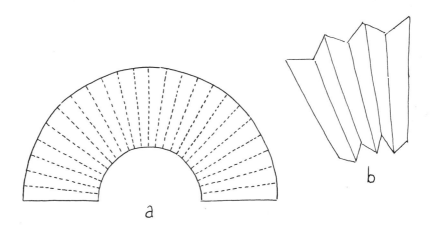

a

b

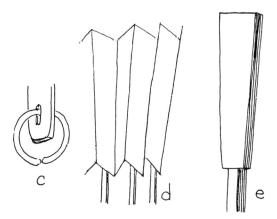

material you use, cut 12 strips as long as the radius. Attach the ends with a wire ring on one side (c). Glue one strip to back of first pleat, and then to every other pleat as in the illustration (d). Glue a strip of cardboard to outside of first and last pleats (e). Decorate this fan with paint.

CHINESE FAN

Cut two equal pieces of thick cardboard about 1 inch wide and 4½ inches long. Cover each piece with black-coated paper (a). Having drawn and cut the shape shown (b) cover and decorate both sides of fan, and glue between the two handle pieces, pressing them together until the glue has dried and set (c).

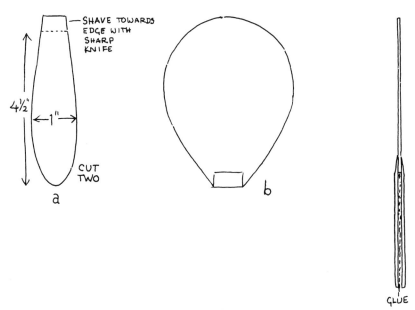

CHAPTER 11

PICTURES, COLLAGES AND DECORATIONS

Personal art has applications, of course, in all the areas of family living, and once people have embarked on projects of creating things for the decoration of their living quarters, they will learn not to expect a Picasso.

Paper is the beginning of pictures of many kinds. The first we will look at are pictures in sculpture, three-dimensional pictures. As a beginning, build up pieces of cut, scored, and folded paper. This type of paper work is usually done with white bristol board or other drawing paper of crisp and bendable quality. Any colors may be used so long as they look well together. Use very sharp tools for clean-cut look. As the subject of the picture must be chosen by its creator, only an example can be offered here.

 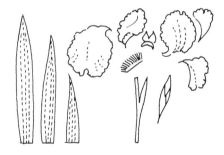

CUT OUT SHADED AREAS

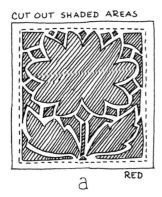

a RED

b ORANGE

c YELLOW AND GREEN

CUNA INDIAN PICTURES

An interesting way to make a paper picture is to follow the Cuna Indian reverse appliqués. The method can be used with the advantage that cutting out the designs through each layer completes the work (no sewing). Start by sketching a design of four or five colors. Then take four or five layers of different-colored papers, and make all sheets the same size in accordance with the size of the design. Keeping in mind the frame, leave ½ inch margin on all sides. The paper should be of a quality easy to cut with scissors, and should be opaque for best effect. Draw first cut-out on outer layer (first color), and cut out pieces which will have another color (a). Then draw or mark pieces to be cut out of second and third colors b and c). Continue in this way to the last layer, but do not cut through the last layer. Now the picture is ready for framing.

CUT-OUT PICTURES

Lace-like cut-out pictures and silhouette cut-out pictures have an old-fashioned look that gains much by comparison, and has its own special applications with respect to memorializing family figures and special occasions in early American art. Because it has the feeling of the moment in time, sad or nostalgic feelings are evoked when observing the incredibly intricate cut-outs depicting the tombstone (preferably with urn) and willow tree of a loved one.

Marriage ceremonies were among the best occasions for memorializing with some tangible object, preferably artistic, and of course it would be especially elegant to display a cut-out of fine quality with a portrait-silhouette of the bride and groom. Often the artist would make use of multiple cutting for most of the design, but made exquisite details separately, going so far as to cut lettering of minute delicacy.

One wonders whether anybody would now take the time and patience to cut detailed pictures of this kind, but surely the fun of trying it is worthwhile, and sometimes the cutting is not as difficult as it seems.

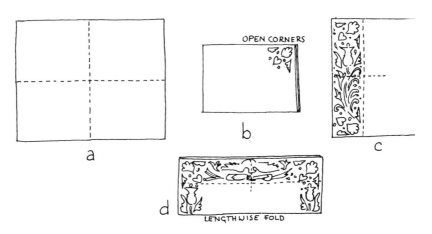

Take in hand a thin, crisp easy-to-cut paper of the size you have decided upon. Fold it in half two times, and sketch your design on one side. Cut through the four layers (a). This will be your corner design. Unfold paper, and refold the side pieces together (b). Cut a basic design for the sides. Now do the same with the top and bottom (c). Finish with all the detail you wish to add by snipping edges, pricking holes of various sizes, and cutting such things as scrolls in the solid pieces (d).

COLLAGES

This is another term for glue-ups or paste-ups, which are essentially the same. In constructing a collage, take a piece of paper or board of fairly heavy quality, and sketch your design on it lightly; or draw inspiration for a true abstraction from the paper you will glue on it. Take tissue papers of random sizes and shapes, and glue them on the board. Use white glue that dries nearly invisible. With brushes and crumpled paper towels tamp down the paper, and use your imagination to achieve various effects. Use lots of glue in some places, and just enough to hold the paper in others.

Real collages can be made using all sorts of cut-outs: scrapbook material, reproductions, playing cards, fancy papers, interesting stickers, and all the rest. Try to express a particular feeling in the way you glue the cut-out objects to a background. When done you may have a picture to be displayed, or a tray decoration to be used under glass. This kind of paper work could also be used for *découpage*. *Découpage* is a form of collage, and refers today to a purely decorative craft of using paper cut-outs for wall hangings, or for covering the surfaces of trays, boxes, table tops, panels of screens and the like.

DECORATIONS

For Easter, so many excellent commercial decorations are available that only a little room is left for original creations, yet these will have a certain superiority. Off to baskets and Easter bunnies!

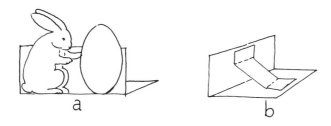

Cut out bunny or egg-and-flower patterns. Place markers can be made either by gluing a cut-out or sticker bunny (or egg or flowers) to a small folded card (a) or to a supported card (b). These tend to stand more erect than the first type.

BIRTHDAYS

For birthday parties almost all of the paper work in earlier chapters may be of interest. Make paper flowers and hang them from the ceiling with ribbons. Make aprons of crepe paper for the little girls and their guests. Make animals of paper, and march them around a young man's birthday cake. Make garlands or twisted streamers, and drape them from the center of the ceiling to the tops of the walls for a cupola effect. Streamers are available commercially, but can be made easily by cutting three-inch slices off packages of crepe paper. Stretch the edges a bit for a slight ruffle, and twist the "ribbon" a bit as you are draping it (c).

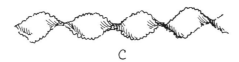

WEDDINGS

For special effects make large white and green bouquets of paper flowers and leaves. Large fronds of white fantasy flowers may be combined with silver or gold-foil paper flowers, and all put together with green leaves and large paper bows to decorate a place where a wedding ceremony might take place (d).

CHAPTER 12
HOLIDAYS AND HOLY DAYS

Christmas was originally Christ Mass, celebrating the birthday of Jesus Christ, and this is ever its central meaning and true significance, whatever trimmings may be added in terms of gayety and self-indulgence. However, it is a birthday party, and are not such parties customarily given over to frivolity? Historically, holy days have tended to be solemn in the morning, jolly at mid-day, and frequently riotous in the evening. Inquiring into tradition, we find that on most of the Christmas days during twenty centuries, pious folk—almost everybody—dressed in their best for attending church in the morning (perhaps a moment after midnight) and then went off to celebrate.

Decorations for the yuletide season vary from stars and snowflakes to candle holders and things of religious meaning such as crèches and triptychs.

STARS

To make a pinwheel star, glue two squares of paper together, first draw and then cut out a pinwheel as in illustration (a). Use two bright colors or foil paper, such as a combination of red and gold foil paper. Make another pinwheel in the same way of perhaps green and silver. Cut notches as illustrated. Overlap the wings of the pinwheel, alternating one wing from each pinwheel, and hooking each notch to the next wing (b). Glue embossed foil ornaments to the centers, attaching a string for use in hanging the pinwheel (c).

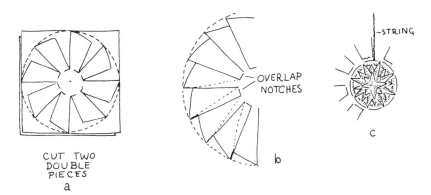

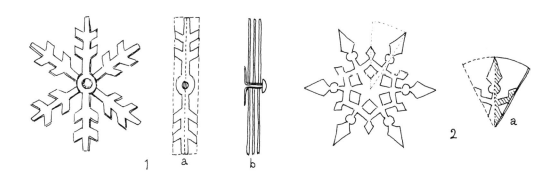

1   a   b   2   a

SNOWFLAKES

All snowflakes are as different from one another as fingerprints. However, all of them are hexagonal, that is to say 6-pointed or 6-sided. Within these limitations the variations are infinite.

One kind of snowflake (1) can be made by taking three equal strips of bristol board or similar board, and drawing the desired design on the top strip (a). Now cut out the design with a very sharp knife (X-Acto). Make a hole in the center of each strip, and join the three strips with an envelope clip (b). Make many of these, and hang them at different levels (using thread) on a Christmas tree or in a window.

Another kind of snowflake (2) is made by cutting a circle of bond paper or thin drawing paper. Fold the circle in half twice, and then fold the paper in thirds. Cut a design so that the folded edges are the centers of the points (a). Unfold and flatten and hang by a thread.

SUNBURST STAR

Fold a circle of foil paper into pleats, and fold the circle about 8 times. Then refold to make pleats (a). Cut irregular points (b). Make two, and attach them in the centers to a small piece of styrofoam, using wire, and finish with a small Christmas ornament. Twist the wires to form a hook for hanging (c).

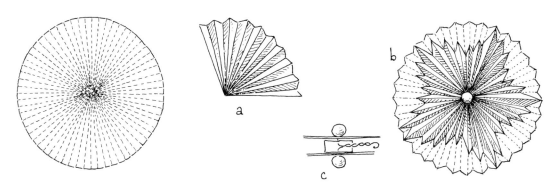

a   b   c

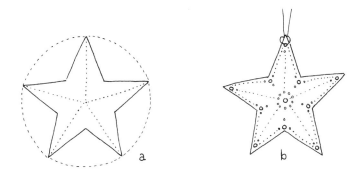

WINDOW STAR

Cut a five-pointed star out of stiff paper. Score and crease points (a) with awl, and pin-prick holes in a design along all edges and folds (b). Hang finished star in window or other place where it will get back-lighting.

SEGMENT STAR

Cut five identical stars of brightly colored paper (such as coated paper), and fold each star in half (a). Glue the back sides of the stars together (b) trim any surplus paper off edges.

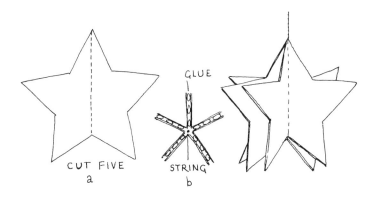

PIXIE ANGEL

Cut a circle of fancy printed paper. Fold it in half and again 3 more times. Unfold and refold into pleats (a). Using the same paper, cut a one-

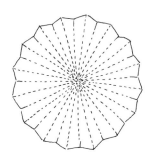

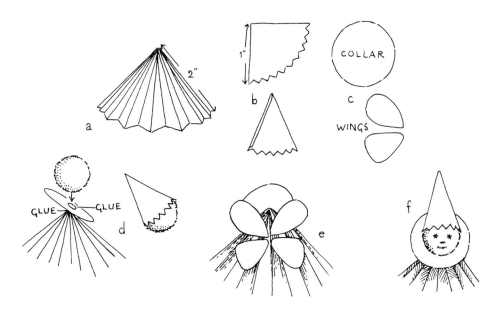

quarter round to make a cone hat. Pink the edge (b). Cut out of white bristol a small circle for a collar, and two sets of wings as in pattern (c).

Glue the collar to the point of the pleated cone. When the glue is dry, add a small cotton head and the hat (d). Glue the wings to a pleat in the back (e). Mark tiny features on the head with ink or felt marker (f).

SCULPTED ANGEL

Pleat the gown of gold or other coated paper. Staple one end (a). Make two cone sleeves (one-quarter circle cone) and glue them to the stapled end of gown (b). Cut two wings as in pattern of double piece of bristol or other drawing paper. Cut feathers for extra dimension. Glue the wings to back of gown (c). Glue cotton head or commercial angel head to top of gown (d).

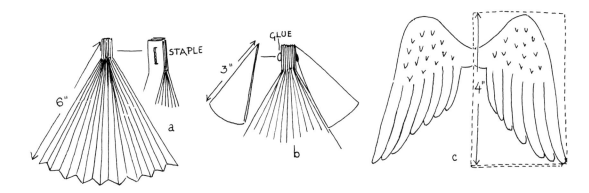

Make fringe of gold foil paper for hair (e). Glue to head. Cut bangs, and curl the fringe with back of knife or scissors. Make a crown or halo by cutting an embossed gold medallion to fit head. Cut out the center of medallion, and cut small tabs (f). Glue the tabs to the heads (g). Add bits of embossed gold edging and paper lace as decoration around edges of gown and sleeves.

CIRCLE ANGEL

Make these of a circle of foil paper or thin white bristol board. Start by drawing a circle on the wrong side of the paper. Draw angels as in pattern (a). Cut out and hook notches (b). For security, staple the lower edge (c). Add features, hair and crown and any other decorations.

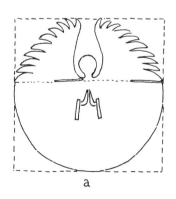

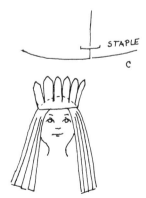

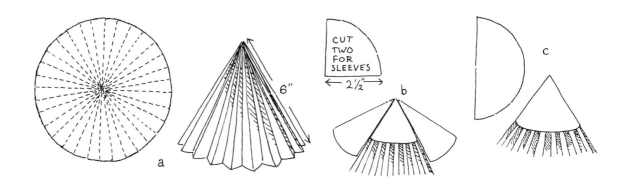

CONE ANGEL

Cut a circle of gift wrap or other printed paper, and of the same paper make two sleeves of one-quarter circle cones. Fold and pleat circle for gown (a). Glue sleeves in place (b). Slip ½ circle cone over top of dress and glue before gluing on sleeves (c). Add a head and decorations.

ANOTHER CONE ANGEL

Very small angels are charming for perching all over a Christmas tree. For the heads, use beads (wooden ones if you can find them) and gold thread for hair and halo. Make a one-third circle cone of crisp coated

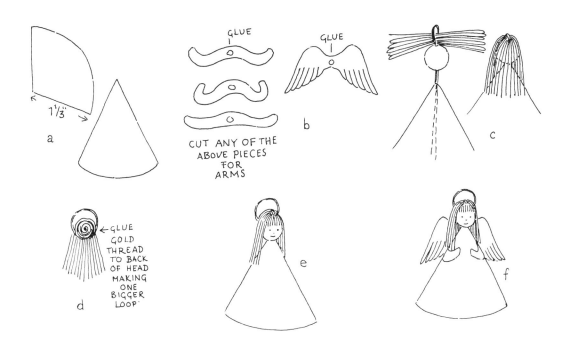

paper, printed paper or foil paper (a). Make arms and wings of interesting colors as in pattern (b). Run a wire through cone point, then through bead and over thread which has been looped about ten times, and then back through bead (c). Make a halo as in illustration (d). Cut bangs, and trim hair. Draw tiny features on face (e). Glue wings and arms in place (f).

TREES

Make a cone of dark green coated paper or any dark green light-weight board, the cone being a one-third circle. Make a stand of a dowel slightly longer than the cone, and a disc of wood or styrofoam or three layers of corrugated board glued together (a). Pink the edge of the cone with pinking shears if the paper is thin enough. Otherwise, use scissors to make points. Make three sizes of flat stars (see below) and space them around tree in tiers, smallest ones at the top (b). This little tree should have stars made of straw, but straw-colored paper or Japanese veneer paper will do just as well when cut in strips. Each star, then, is built up of pairs of strips. Each strip is ribbon-cut at ends. The pairs of strips can be regular or irregular, short or long (c). Use red thread to tie two pairs together in the center as in illustra-

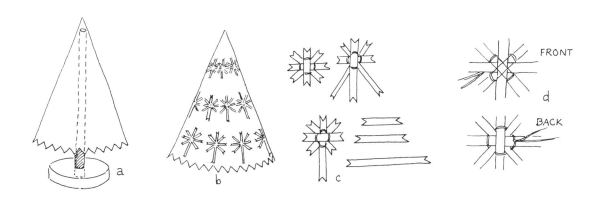

tion. These same stars may be used to decorate a big coniferous Christmas tree, in which case leave the red thread long enough to make a loop so that the stars can be hung on the branches of the tree (d).

GEOMETRICAL TREE

Cut two pieces of thin poster board or other paper of similar stiffness, as in drawing. Fold each in half lengthwise, and cut notches as indicated (a). Fit the pieces together, and glue a short piece of dowel or rolled board

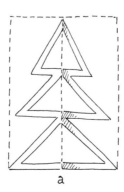

a

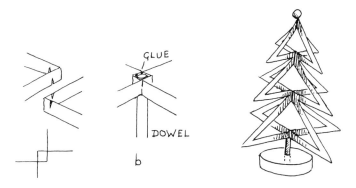

(roll strip of paper around pencil with glue) to center of bottom tier (b). Secure other end of stem in disc of wood, styrofoam, or corrugated board (three layers glued together) and top the tree with a small Christmas ball.

CONE TREE

Make a one-third circle cone of dark green paper or board (a). Cut many leaves of various shapes of two or three colors of crepe paper (b). Glue the leaves in spirals around cone until the entire cone is covered (c). Add tiny Christmas balls. Prick holes in cone, and stick wire of the balls to the inside of cone. (For the making of other trees see Chapter 6.)

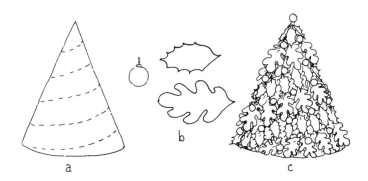

SEGMENTED BALL

Cut twenty equal circles of several colors of foil paper or other crisp paper. Fold all the circles in half (a). Glue the half circles together back to

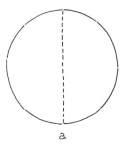

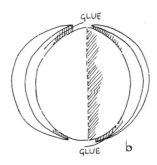

back (b) being careful to have all the fold-edges meet in the center. When all half circles are glued and dry, trim off any uneven edges, and fold segments out to form ball. Hang with a thread.

GEOMETRIC BALL

Cut two circles of brightly colored paper. Glue them together back to back. Mark concentric circles lightly on one side, and then cut through both layers leaving a narrow axis in the middle uncut (a). Fold entire circle in half, and then fold every other ring, one half up, and one half down so that alternate rings are at right angles to each other (b). Hang with a thread.

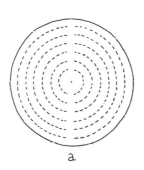
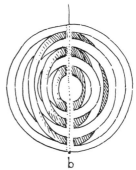

SPIRAL ORNAMENT

Cut two circles of thin bristol board or similar paper, preferably in bright colors. Cut spiral strips as in pattern, always leaving a margin of about ½ inch uncut around edge and a circle in the center 1 inch in diameter (a). Glue the circle rims together (b). Attach a small ball or bell or other decoration to a string (c). Run the string through the bottom center. Through the slots in the upper half of ornament make a knot in the string, and then run it through the top center (d). This will prevent the finished ornament from sagging.

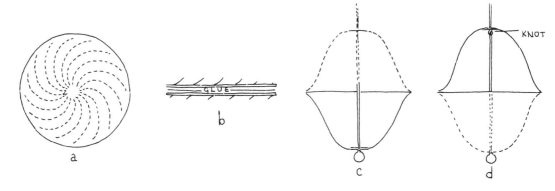

TISSUE BALL

Cut forty equal circles out of tissue paper. Fold them all in half (a). Thread all the corners as indicated (b). Tie and knot one end. Cut the

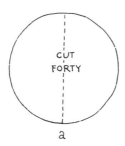

a

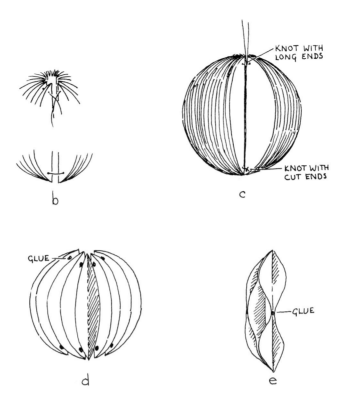

thread end. Tie and knot the other thread but leave the thread ends long enough for use as a hanging loop (c). Now glue pieces of the tissue paper together, two and two, continuing until all are mated (d). Now glue the same pieces at the other end, two and two, together. To finish the ball, switch to gluing the alternating two-and-two's all the way around the middle of the ball (e).

ANOTHER TISSUE BALL

Take thirty equal circles of many colors of tissue paper (or all of one color). Cut each circle into eight sections, leaving about one inch in the center uncut (a). Wrap each section around a knitting needle or similar shape, and twist the end firmly (b). When all the circles have been treated this way, thread through the centers, and pull tight and knot. Put a small piece of cardboard at each end of tissues before threading (c). Fluff up the ball like a pom-pom (d).

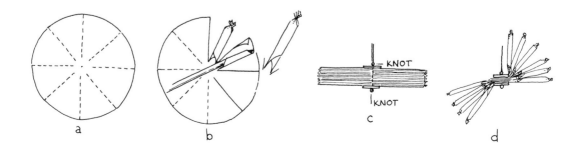

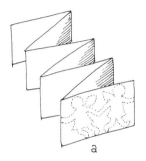
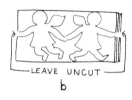

LEAVE UNCUT

b

GLUE

c

a

ANGEL GARLAND

Take a strip of paper, making the length 16 times greater than the width. (If the width is an inch, the length is 16 inches). Fold into eight equal parts back and forth (a). Draw the angels on the top fold, and cut out, making certain that hands are not cut (b). Unfold. If the garlands are to be longer, cut the same design of more than 16 folds, and the length can be infinitely extended by gluing the end angels' hands together (c).

CHAINS

Cut many strips of colorful paper, preferably thin, about ½ inch wide and 5 inches long. Make a loop by gluing ends of one strip together (a). Loop the next strip through the first, glue ends, and continue the process with the remaining strips (b). It is handy to use gummed paper which comes in many colors.

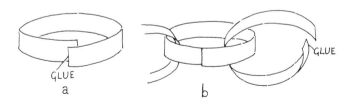

DIAMOND CHAIN

It is helpful to cut many of the different parts of the diamonds before starting to make them one at a time. To this end cut two strips of the same length and about 1 inch wide out of stiff colored paper or thin board (a). Cut four fans of cellophane or tissue paper, and gather at one end.

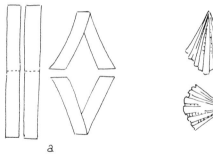

a

STAPLE

b

Make the fans all the same size—about three-quarters of the length of the folded strip. Staple two fans between the open ends of the strips (b). Then staple the other two fans in the folded ends of the strips. When you have a large number of these diamonds, staple the folded ends together (c).

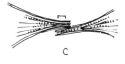

c

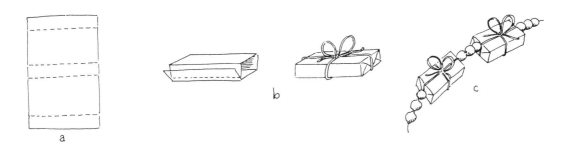

LITTLE BOXES CHAIN

Make many of these tiny boxes to string into long garlands for hanging on the Christmas tree. Each box should be about 1½ inches long when finished. Cut the strip for the boxes 3½ inches long of thin cardboard or thick paper as in pattern (a). Fold on dotted lines. Wrap each box in paper such as may fit in with your decorative scheme. Use as many different colors and prints as you like. Place small spots of glue where needed. Now tie each little parcel with brightly-colored string or yarn (b). Using a darning needle and thin string, make a garland by stringing a few (three or four) Christmas beads, then a tiny package, alternating in this way to the desired length (c).

FLOWER CHAIN

Cut six equal strips of thin-colored board or thick paper. Make a fan of tissue or cellophane to fit each looped strip (a). Gather one end of fan, and staple between loop ends. Glue the pointed ends of six loops together to form flower (b). A garland of these flowers may be made by stapling two of the flowers together in the middle of two corresponding loops (c).

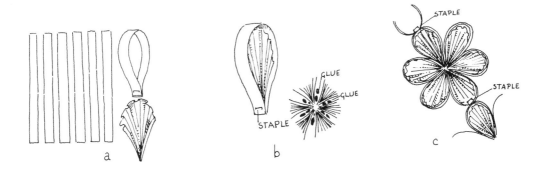

HANGING BELL CHAIN

Make many cone bells of one-third circles of paper. Turn them to shape, and fasten with glue or staple (a). Now take a narrow ribbon or a piece of yarn or string, and make a knot at one end. String on a cone bell. A few inches above bell, make another knot, string on another bell, and continue the process as long as you wish (b).

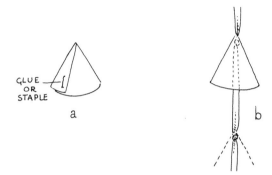

BELLS AND CANDLES

Start by cutting bell-shaped pieces of paper, crisp and brightly colored, and not forgetting the foil papers (a). Fold each piece in half and with Elmer's or a similar glue, glue the folded edges together (b). While gluing the edges together, put a ribbon in the middle (running the length of the bell) with a piece at the bottom hanging free to attach to a small Christmas ball that will be the clapper, and enough at the top to use in hanging the bell.

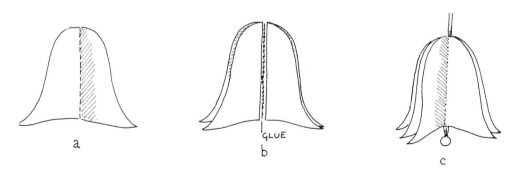

CANDLE HOLDERS

Small candle holders can be made of cardboard. From such board cut a strip about 1 inch wide and long enough to go around the candle with enough extra for an overlap (a). Before gluing, score on dotted line for use in cutting tabs. Roll strip around finger or pencil to form cylinder. Glue

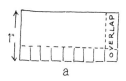

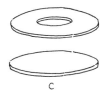
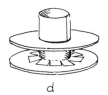

together the overlapping pieces, and hold until the glue sets (b). Now cut two discs of cardboard about 2 inches in diameter. Out of the center of one, cut a round of the same diameter as the cylinder (c). Glue tabs of the cylinder to the whole disc. Then slip the one with the hole over the cylinder, and glue together (d). Decorate the holder with gold-foil-embossed edging, stars, ruffles, or any other frippery that fancy may suggest.

CANDLE RUFF

Make the ruff in much the same way as a meat ruff (page 130), but much longer. Fold a strip of foil paper or colored paper in half lengthwise inside out, and cut a fringe (a). Unfold and refold right side out, now wrap around candle several times and glue end (b). Finish lower edge with embossed foil edging (c). If the candle is to be used only as a decoration, it and the ruff may be anchored anywhere in liquid wax, but if it is to be placed in a candlestick, the ruff will rest on the rim of the candlestick holder (d).

The fuller the ruff, the more spectacular the effect, especially when paper flowers and such delicate greenery are used to decorate the candlestick.

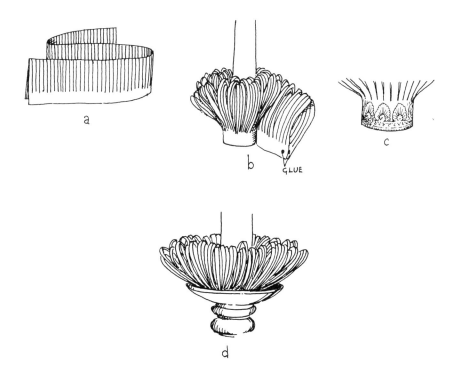

DECORATED BOTTLES

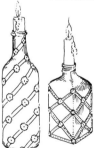

Candles and bottles have a certain affinity, and there is art in the decorating of the bottles to show off the candles. To these bottles glue strips of colored paper or ribbon or embossed foil edging with floral stickers or gold medallions.

CRECHES

Christmas is symbolized in many ways, one of the most beautiful being the journey of the Wise Men from afar to see the newborn child of whom prophets had said that he would redeem the world and open up the way to

172

eternal life. Artists have the faculty of enabling people to see such complicated things at a glance, and their way has been mostly that ancient one of
showing the simple parents with their child in the manger with all the world
adoring. The crèche is the central symbol of Christmas.

To make a crèche, start with a triptych which stands by itself, or a little
lean-to stable, or arrange the figures without any surrounding building on
a mantle or table.

TRIPTYCH

This is a basic structure for which you cut a piece of medium bristol
board twice as long as it is wide, and score as indicated on dotted lines (a).
Fold the two side pieces to center of middle piece. Now cut a second piece
of bristol board, and score it as indicated on dotted lines, and fold (b).
Draw figures on second piece and cut out (c). Draw figures on the back
of the first piece, and cut where indicated (d). Now decorate by making
clothing and features with bits of paper and trimmings of various kinds.
Glue on layer upon layer of details. Marvelous effects can be accomplished
using the many shades of tissue paper.

When the pieces are properly decorated, glue them together where
indicated (e). Fold the pieces in the directions shown, and close the
triptych. The outside can be decorated with appropriate motifs (f). A small
version can be sent by mail when closed and put in an envelope, or a
larger one can be used for display standing open on a table, shelf, or
mantel.

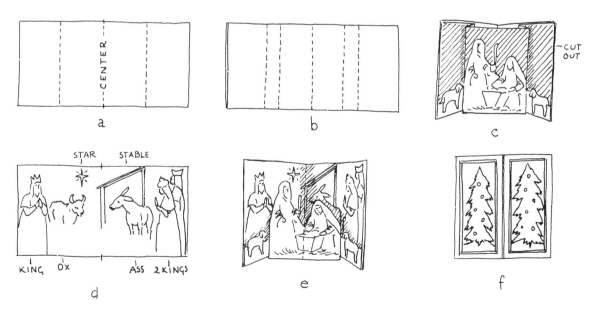

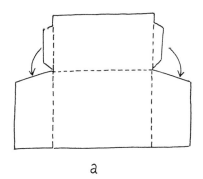

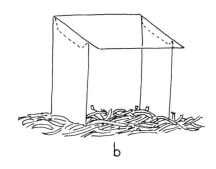

a

b

LEAN-TO STABLE

As a beginning, cut a piece of cardboard of the proportions shown in pattern (a). Fold and glue the tabs as indicated (b). Use colored poster board or paint the stable later. Covering plain cardboard is possible, but should be done before cutting. Set the stable in sand, and use shredded tissue paper for straw. Make cone figures or combine various shapes of folded paper or use cut-out figures.

CONE CRECHE FIGURES

Make various figures by changing the cone size (a). Make cut-out features, and glue them to the cone tips. Make a cradle of bristol or poster board (b). Make the child of a cylinder of bristol board (c). Again use tissue paper and crepe paper for clothing, not forgetting such ornaments as embossed foil edgings. Shredded tissue paper will be good for lining the cradle (d).

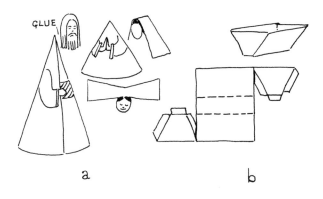

a

b

174

c

d

FOLDED PAPER FIGURES

Draw the figures on heavy drawing board, and add the supports as illustrated (a). Cut the details (b). Cut out the figures, and stand them up. Make the animals as in Chapter 7.

FRONT
OF
FIGURE

CUT-OUT FIGURES

Many Christmas cards of other years are still as beautiful as ever—and sometimes of even more interest than they were originally. The figures can be cut out and glued to little stands made of thin cardboard (a) or cut-out figures may be made of thin board—and painted or decorated with paper (b).

GLUE FRAME TO
LEGS AND BODY

GLUE TO
BACK OF
FIGURE

GLUE

GLUE

Ours is a wonderful world, and paper art helps to make it so. On land and sea and in the air, paper art is everywhere. People flying kites, flying planes, and shooting off rockets—all must acknowledge their indebtedness to paper art. A drawing on paper or a folding of paper is where it all began, charting a pathway to the Moon, to the other planets, or to the distant stars.